PRAISE FOR G[...]

"Engaging from the first page. In a conversational style, David Hajduk, draws you in to explore some of life's big questions and pulls back the veil so that you can catch a glimpse of God's glorious plan. He succeeds in the challenging task of making John Paul II's theology of the body not only accessible to teens, but also attractive and fascinating, a path to follow. A biblically-based antidote to the relativism and subjectivism that surrounds teens today. Complete with discussion questions and quotes for reflection. A fabulous resource for religion classes, youth groups, retreats."

— Sr. Mary Elizabeth Wusinich, SV, Vicar General of the Sisters of Life

"In his updated book, *God's Plan for You*, David Hajduk's crisp and engaging writing style brings to life the theology of the body in an a way which 'thinks with the Church' and provides a roadmap to purity and virtue."

— Allan F. Wright, author; adjunct professor of theology and Catholic studies, Seton Hall University

"In his theology of the body, Saint John Paul II shares deep truths about the significance of our existence, our bodies, and our relationships. Our culture, loudly and brazenly, speaks lies to students daily. Communicating the beautiful truth of the theology of the body and the vocation God himself has placed on every person can be a daunting task, but David Hajduk has accomplished it brilliantly. He tackles all of the 'tough' issues with clarity and grace and gives students the opportunity to THINK and assimilate these life-changing values."

—Pam Stenzel, M.A., chastity speaker, author,
Enlighten Communications

"Speaking to both head and heart, David Hajduk has written a book that leaves the reader with the sure and certain conviction: *this is true.*"

—Fr. James Cuddy, OP, STL, pastor,
Saint Joseph's Church, Greenwich Village

"By weaving in modern-day media and humor, Hajduk relates to the reader ... Every teenager should read this book as 'how-to' guide to growing up and finding love by first finding our roots in God."

—Kaylin Koslosky, co-founder, www.restoreyourcrown.com; blogger at www.chastityproject.com

"David Hajduk's approach bears the marks of many questions from challenging youth and lessons learned from his own fatherhood. I truly appreciate how he helps us understand JPII within the pastoral context of *The Joy of the Gospel.* A great read for those who want a common-sense approach."

—Fr. Agustino Torres, CFR, founder,
Corazón Puro and Latinos Por la Vida

"Already one of my favorite theology of the body reads, Hajduk's refresh of God's Plan for You elevates it to 'must-read' status for our 'This is my body/This is not my body' world."

—Damon Owens, Executive Director, joytob.org; former Executive Director, Theology of the Body Institute

"David Hajduk is an enthusiastic, reliable, and accessible communicator of Saint John Paul's theology of the body for teens. I highly recommend this work."

—Dr. Petroc Willey, Director, Office of Catechetics, Franciscan University of Steubenville

"*God's Plan for You: Life, Love, Marriage and Sex* is a timely and most welcome book. In language that speaks directly to young people, the author gently leads his readers into a healthy understanding of human sexuality. Pope John Paul II's theology of the body is made not only accessible, but inviting for young people. The author's use of Scripture helps the reader connect theology and revelation. His ample use of anecdotes and examples anchors the truths of faith in life. A great book. A most useful tool."

— Most Rev. Arthur J. Serratelli, Bishop of Paterson, New Jersey

"I really enjoyed reading *God's Plan for You*. In it, David takes the beautiful teachings of our Church and the words of Pope John Paul the Great and puts them in terms that all can understand. This book beautifully weaves together God's great design for life, love, marriage, and sex. I appreciated the fact that David always refers back to Scripture and the *Catechism of the Catholic Church* as the basis for each of his points. Young people today are struggling to hear and really live the truth. This book boldly and yet lovingly lays out God's truth. I thank David for giving me a great resource which I can use with the campus ministry program that my wife and I lead in our home town."

— Tony Melendez
Composer and musician

"In a world that bombards all of us, and particularly young people, with deceptive and confusing messages about the gift of our sexuality, David has put together an indispensable resource. His humor and personality shine through even as he deals with difficult topics, and the message is right on the money. He has brought both The Theology of the body and Church teaching in the *Catechism* into clear focus and everyday language. I am inspired by this book, knowing the power that it has to change lives."

— Steve Angrisano
Youth minister, singer, and songwriter

God's Plan for You

Life, Love, Marriage & Sex

SECOND EDITION

By David Hajduk

Foreword to the Second Edition by Sr. Helena Burns, FSP

Pauline
BOOKS & MEDIA

Boston

Nihil Obstat: Christopher P. Klofft, S.T.D.   *Imprimatur:* ✠ Seán Cardinal O'Malley, O.F.M. Cap.
Archbishop of Boston
June 30, 2017

Library of Congress Cataloging-in-Publication Data

Names: Hajduk, David (David Charles), author.
Title: God's plan for you : life, love, marriage & sex / by David Hajduk ;
  foreword by Helena Burns, FSP.
Description: Boston, MA : Pauline Books & Media, 2018. | Includes
  bibliographical references.
Identifiers: LCCN 2017017673| ISBN 9780819831392 (pbk.) | ISBN 0819831395
  (pbk.)
Subjects: LCSH: Marriage--Religious aspects--Catholic Church. |
  Sex--Religious aspects--Catholic Church. | Catholic Church--Doctrines. |
  Teenagers--Sexual behavior. | Teenagers--Conduct of life. |
  Teenagers--Religious life.
Classification: LCC BX2250 .H26 2018 | DDC 248.8/3--dc23
LC record available at https://lccn.loc.gov/2017017673

Published by Pauline Books & Media, 50 Saint Paul's Avenue, Boston, MA 02130-3491

Printed in the U.S.A.

www.pauline.org

Pauline Books & Media is the publishing house of the Daughters of St. Paul, an international congregation of women religious serving the Church with the communications media.

1 2 3 4 5 6 7 8 9   22 21 20 19 18

For my father,
the "man behind the man,"
who by his words and example has taught me
what it means to love as God loves.

CONTENTS

FOREWORD TO THE SECOND EDITION

It isn't easy being in your teens. You couldn't pay me enough to relive those years. But I not only survived, I thrived. Why? Because, God. I got to know God when I was fifteen (I didn't really believe in God before then). Knowing God meant that my world got a whole lot bigger. I got to be part of something bigger than just my little self and my little world with all my problems that seemed so overwhelming at the time. And best of all, I came to understand that God LOVES me and that this earth isn't all there is. God is waiting for me in heaven, and he's more excited for me to go there and be with him than I am.

So what does knowing God have to do with *your* life? Everything. You came from God (who is Love) and are going back to God (who is Love), and life is short. It's illogical to try to live our lives without God (or basically just ignoring God, which is called "practical atheism"). It doesn't make sense not to let God, our Creator, Redeemer, and Sanctifier into our lives: the only One who can truly help us, who'll always be there for us, who never gives up on us.

"Theology of the Body" is a primary, indispensable way to get to know God—through our own bodies. If we are made "in the image of God," then our bodies are theology textbooks. Did you, perhaps, think it was only your *soul* that was made in the image of God? Nope. We are one person: body and soul. We can't have only one part of us made in the image of God. In fact, an "image" is something you can *see*. Can you see your soul? No. Can you see your body? Yes. *Boom*. We need to learn to read and hear "the language of the body" to understand who we are and what the meaning of our life is.

If we don't know who we are, we'll spend our lives searching for our identity, online and offline. Satan always offers us false identities. It's what he does (identity theft). Starting in the Garden of Eden, he told Adam and Eve that they were *not* beloved children of God, that there were *not* like God, that God was *not* good. Satan was telling them to trust *him* instead of God.

Probably all our lives we've heard: "We're all children of God!" Even people with very little faith usually have a sense of that and can agree with that. BUT—who teaches us to *grow up in God*, to become *men and women of God*? We may have had faith in God when we were little, but then puberty hits. Whoa. Suddenly we have all kinds of new feelings, and not just sexual urges. We also begin to feel a deep ache, a deep longing to love and be loved at our deepest levels. And who the heck is helping us with *that*?

So often it's at puberty that we may begin to drift away from God because our childish faith no longer matches our new reality. But this shouldn't be! It's our capacity to know and to love that makes us *most* like God, and this is expressed in a profound way through our sexuality. As we mature, we grow in our ability to participate in God's love and life in a new, fuller, and mature way. At the time in our lives when we most need God, we may tend to think he only loved us when we were little kids and didn't have all kinds of sexual feelings, problems, and weren't making sexual mistakes. Nothing could be further from the truth. Because this ache, this longing, is not only for another person who will love us for a lifetime. We are longing for Ultimate Love, for God, who will love us forever. God doesn't just love part of us! He loves us with all our sexual hang-ups, and he wants to help us navigate them so that they can even become a way of sharing in his love and his life—so that the body will reveal all of its beauty to us. When we try to "use" beauty for our own selfish gratification, it hides its secrets, because beauty can't be used.

Theology of the body is all about teaching us how to grow up *in* God and toward God—not away from God—to the "full stature of Christ" (Eph 4:13). God wants to talk to you, face to face, as the amazing adult man or woman you're becoming: "Come now, and let us reason together" (Is 1:18). You are precious to him.

Our culture hasn't given up on love, sex, beauty, the body, or relationships. But do you think the culture knows what all these things really are, really mean, and how to best live them? You can be the generation that turns a "culture of death" into a culture of life, love, and beauty.

Theology of the body isn't about what you *can't* have, it's about what you *can* have. Theology of the body isn't a bunch of *external* requirements imposed on us from the outside. It's about what the *internal* requirements of true love and true sex challenge us to, *if* we want to get the most out of them.

Theology of the body is not a bunch of rules. Theology of the body doesn't say: "*Do* this, don't *do* that." It says: "This is who you *are*. Now go forth and *live* it." And don't forget, God loves you. He is for you, not against you. He's on your side, in your corner. Deal with it.

Sr. Helena Burns, FSP[1]

FOREWORD TO THE FIRST EDITION

Saint John Paul II changed my life.

When I first heard of his theology of the body, I was a senior in college and a "nice Catholic girl." By that, I mean that I went to Mass on Sunday and tried to avoid committing the really big sins. I followed the rules because I knew they were the rules. I have to admit, I wasn't entirely sure *why* they were the rules, or why I was supposed to follow them. I knew I wasn't supposed to steal or kill because that hurt people. And I abstained from sexual activity because I didn't want to get pregnant and didn't want to make God mad.

Compelling, but not particularly positive reasons.

All of that changed when a series of four speakers came in to talk to us about John Paul II and the theology of the body. I was completely blown away. I saw "the rules" in a whole new light. God's laws—his morality—are about *love!* He has a plan for our lives and for our bodies. When he says "Thou shalt not . . ." it's because if we "shalt," we'll end up hurting ourselves and hurting our ability to love.

I saw in particular how the Catholic Church's teaching on human sexuality was based on love. We're created for love. We hunger for love. And we think somehow that "making love" will help us to live love.

It doesn't work that way. Living God's plan—chastity —helps us find and live love.

I thought this news was so exciting, I decided I wanted to share it with teenagers. I've been doing that full time ever since.

Saint John Paul II had an amazing gift for conveying the truths of our faith in a beautiful, positive way. He made Christ's love so real and so immediate that rules didn't seem like rules anymore. They are simply a natural response to God's overwhelming love for us.

From the very beginning of my work with teens and chastity, everything I've said or written has been based on the theology of the body. I didn't go out of my way to advertise that fact in the early years of my ministry, because the word "theology" freaked people out. But Saint John Paul II changed even that. Now the theology of the body is actually "cool." People are excited about it; they want to learn about it.

Fortunately, you have an excellent opportunity to do just that. David Hajduk shares my enthusiasm for the work of Saint John Paul II, and he has captured the Holy Father's message in the book you hold in your hands. Take full advantage of this opportunity. Read it. Re-read it. Think about it. Pray to understand it on a deeper and deeper level.

Saint John Paul II's signature phrase was "Be not afraid." I want you to remember that as you read this book. God is madly in love with you. He wants what is best for you. Most of all, God wants to have a relationship with you. He wants you to share eternal happiness with him in heaven.

God is on your side. And that, my friends, is very, very good news.

Read on . . .

Mary Beth Bonacci

ACKNOWLEDGMENTS

I would like to thank the following people and groups of people, who are all truly collaborators in the work you hold in your hands:

Shannon, my wife and true companion, for the life we have built and continue to build together by allowing ourselves, however imperfectly, to be guided by God's plan from "the beginning." Our love story is both the inspiration and richest resource for my writing.

My children, who showed so much excitement about their daddy writing a book, even though it meant days when I may have seemed to spend more time with the computer than with them.

My parents, for always believing that I could accomplish great things if I worked hard, and for being unwavering in their thinking that I'm the best thing since sliced bread.

My friends, who believed in me and who, if they ever got tired of discussing the book, never once let on, especially Catzel LaVecchia and Marie Ryan.

The religious educators and youth ministers who reviewed my initial manuscript, believed in the value of the project, and offered their professional advice, especially Joel Peters, Michael St. Pierre, and Allan Wright.

All the young people I have had the pleasure to teach or minister to over the years, who, whether they knew it or not, were in a way "writing" this book.

Mary Beth Bonacci, for taking time out of her busy schedule to write the foreword.

Pauline Books & Media and their associates—especially Sr. Donna Giaimo, Sr. Marianne Lorraine Trouvé, Sr. Christina Wegendt, and Mr. Steven Colella—for believing in this project, for their expert advice, and for sharing a passion and vision for reaching young people with the life-giving message of God's plan for life, love, marriage, and sex!

And to Saint John Paul II for all he has taught me.

CHAPTER 1

THE COSMIC PREQUEL

*Some Pharisees approached him, and tested him,
saying, "Is it lawful for a man to divorce his wife for
any cause whatever?" He said in reply, "Have you not
read that from the beginning the Creator 'made them
male and female' and said, 'For this reason a man
shall leave his father and mother and be joined to his
wife, and the two shall become one flesh'? So they are
no longer two, but one flesh. Therefore, what God has
joined together, no human being must separate."*

—Matthew 19:3–6 NAB

GOD'S PLAN FOR YOU FROM THE BEGINNING

The first *Star Wars* movie (Episode IV that is) came
out when I was in the first grade, and I eagerly awaited
each subsequent episode. My father and I would stand
in lines that wrapped around the movie theater and
continued for blocks. I had every action figure, as well

as the Darth Vader carrying case. I had all the space-ships. I traded *Star Wars* cards. You get the picture.

So in 1999, when George Lucas began coming out with the prequels, "the story behind the story," I was pumped up beyond your wildest imagination. I imme-diately changed from a thirty-year-old man back into a seven-year-old boy, and all was right with the world. My kids instantly morphed into *Star Wars* junkies. The hours spent jumping around the living room recreat-ing the lightsaber "dual of the fates" between Darth Maul, Qui-Gon Jinn, and Obi-wan Kenobi will be forever etched in our memories. And with the force having been reawakened with the new films, you can only imagine the craze that has overtaken our house once again!

I realize there are a lot of strong opinions out there about the Star Wars prequels, but for me they really helped to shed light on the original three movies. Let's just say that, watching them, I experienced my share of "a-ha" moments: moments when a light bulb went on in my head and I suddenly realized something I hadn't before. Well, when Jesus refers the Pharisees back to "the beginning," to the time when God created human beings and the first human couple, you might say he is reminding them about their "prequel," about the story behind their story. And since their prequel is every-body's prequel—including yours and mine—you could call it *The Cosmic Prequel.*

Why would Jesus want to take the Pharisees and us back to the beginning and remind us of the story behind our story? Because Jesus wants us to understand what our lives are really all about. He wants us to know God's plan for us, and he wants us to see how the amazing gifts of love, marriage, and sex are all part of that plan! I really do believe that Jesus hoped (and still hopes) that

WORD TO THE WISE

Pontificate is a fancy word meaning the Holy Father's time as pope.

doing so would give us some serious "a-ha" moments.

Saint John Paul II hoped so too! That's why, at the beginning of his pontificate, he devoted over five years' worth of general audience teachings to *The Cosmic Prequel* and how it sheds light on love, marriage, and sex. This teaching eventually became known as the **theology of the body**

Did U Know

The custom of the general audience, a weekly teaching given by the Holy Father, was started by Pope Pius IX in the 1870s.

(TOB). In it, he stresses the goodness of the body and how a proper understanding of the body enables us to know what it means to be human and what human sexuality is all about. This brings me to the book you have in your hands.

THE MEANING OF LIFE, LOVE, MARRIAGE, AND SEX, AND THE POPE FROM POLAND

Have you ever wondered what life is all about? Have you ever struggled with finding your place in this world? Have you ever looked in a mirror and been unsure if you like what you see, or even *know* what you see? Have you ever been confused about relationships, sex, or members of the opposite sex? Have you become disillusioned over marriage and family life? Well, you're not alone. When I was a teen, I did my share of questioning, and in my years working with teens I have never met one who hasn't wrestled with these issues on some level.

The teenage years can be difficult, and even more so today. Enormous pressure, high expectations, and an uncertain future with slender job prospects all can be the source of anxiety. We supposedly live in the Information Age, but we're fed so much contradictory information that it's hard to know what to believe about anything.

Then there are those guy-girl relationships. As far as sex goes, who knows what to think anymore? Society seems to treat sex in a very casual way, almost recreationally, and we are encouraged daily to view others (and ourselves) in terms of sexual desirability. Struggles persist with body image, Internet pornography, drug and alcohol use, date rape, sexually transmitted infections, and abortion, though society offers little in terms of concrete solutions to such problems. As the divorce rate continues to increase, many teens look at their own broken families and ask, "Is this the best I can hope for?" More and more young adults are even opting not to marry at all. Disillusionment and regret grow, though we are told we shouldn't have either. All things considered, it's not a very happy or hopeful outlook.

And these elements of modern society can make the message coming from the Church even more counter-cultural, and perhaps incomprehensible, to young people. You may ask yourself: How could an old Polish man who lived in the Vatican for over twenty-six years possibly have known anything about your life, your struggles, your hopes, dreams, or fears? Yet he did. It may surprise you to learn that, as a young man, Saint John Paul II dreamed of becoming a famous actor in the theater. As a young priest, he worked with youth and spent lots of time with them, taking them on canoeing, hiking, and skiing trips (he used to be quite an avid skier). As pope, John Paul II loved to meet with young people from all over the globe at the World Youth Day celebrations every two years. He really did love young people. He really did understand your challenges. And from heaven he really wants *you* to live life to the full and not to fear the future.

NOTABLE QUOTABLE

You are young, and the Pope is old; 82 or 83 years of life is not the same as 22 or 23, but the Pope still fully identifies with your hopes and aspirations. Although I have lived through much darkness, under harsh totalitarian regimes, I have seen enough evidence to be unshakably convinced that no difficulty, no fear is so great that it can completely suffocate the hope that springs eternal in the hearts of the young. You, the young, are our hope. Do not let that hope die! Stake your lives on it!

—Saint John Paul II

In his theology of the body (TOB), Saint John Paul II has provided us with the secret to a full life and a reason to hope for the future. In TOB we find the purpose of our existence and the answers to our most deeply held questions about life, relationships, and sexuality. And it really is some of the most powerful, uplifting, and downright mind-blowing stuff on earth! The TOB exposes as shallow and bogus what a consumerist or purely secular society holds up to us as the "ideal." I only wish that I had learned about it before my mid-twenties. It would have spared me a lot of confusion, pain, and bad choices. That's why I want to introduce it to you. That's precisely why I wrote this book.

HOW TO GET THE MOST FROM THIS BOOK

In the following pages, I have broken the theology of the body down into bite-sized portions. Each chapter begins with an important insight from God's word as the "springboard" for that chapter's theme. Please read it slowly and prayerfully. Then, I offer an introductory example or analogy and present one piece of *The Cosmic Prequel* and what it teaches us about the meaning of life, love, marriage, and sex. Each chapter ends with an "In His Own Words" section containing a quote from Saint John Paul II on that chapter's topic; a "Things to Ponder and Share" section with questions that will help you relate the themes discussed in the chapter to your everyday life; and some suggested reading from the *Catechism of the Catholic Church (CCC)* to help you to "go deeper" if you so choose. All in all, I have written the book like I speak in the hopes that it will read less like a textbook and more like a conversation with a friend.

So, let's take a look at *The Cosmic Prequel*—the story behind our story. Those "a-ha" moments are waiting for us.

JOHN PAUL II
In His Own Words

Those who seek the fulfillment of their own human and Christian vocation in marriage are called first of all to make of this "theology of the body" . . . the content of their lives and behavior.

(TOB 23:5)

THINGS TO PONDER AND SHARE

1. Understanding "the story behind our story" helps us to understand and appreciate our story. Have you ever wondered about your family history: where your relatives came from and when, what perhaps earlier generations did when they got to this country, etc.? Ask your parents or grandparents

about it the next time you get a chance. You'll be fascinated by the stories!

2. What are the reasons Jesus takes the Pharisees (and us) back to "the beginning"?

3. What pressures face teens today? How do you cope with them?

4. What is the prevalent attitude in society toward relationships, sex, and marriage? What are some subtle and not so subtle examples that demonstrate it?

5. What is the role of the Pope? Have you ever imagined any of the popes caring for you personally? Why or why not?

6. What are some of the questions you or other young people today might have about love, marriage, and sex? What do you hope to gain from reading this book?

·· READ THE CATECHISM OF THE CATHOLIC CHURCH ····

nos. 1701, 1602–1603

CHAPTER 2

THE KEY TO A RICH LIFE

"Do not lay up for yourselves treasures on earth, where moth and rust consume and where thieves break in and steal, but lay up for yourselves treasures in heaven, where neither moth nor rust consumes and where thieves do not break in and steal. For where your treasure is, there will your heart be also."

—Matthew 6:19–21

LIFE'S MOST IMPORTANT QUESTIONS

The movie *It's a Wonderful Life* starring Jimmy Stewart brings a tear to my eye every time I watch it. If you have never seen it, don't worry—it's on TV at least a hundred times from Thanksgiving to Christmas. It tells the story of George Bailey, a man of duty and charity who meets hard times. He stands to lose his reputation, family welfare, and business because his archrival, a heartless and crooked old miser named Mr. Potter, wants to ruin him. Unlike George, Mr. Potter has no concern for the hardworking men and women in town and views them solely as a means of profit. Desperate, George begins to think that he is worth more dead than alive and that everyone would be better off if he had never been born. Well, through the intervention of a second-class angel trying to earn his wings, George gets the chance to see what life would have been like had he never existed, and he realizes all the wonderful things he has done with his life. The movie ends at George's house, with all the people helped by George rallying together to help him in his time of need. George's brother, Harry, shows up and proposes a toast: "To my brother, George Bailey— the richest man in town!"

Everyone wants to have a rich life. Everyone wants to "store up treasure for themselves." However, the real question is: What makes a person rich? At some point in life, everyone will have to answer this question for him- or herself—and the answer will ultimately determine how full his or her life will be.

At its core, the question "What makes a person rich?" inquires into the meaning of life and the purpose of human existence. In a sense, it asks two separate yet related questions: "Who am I?" and "What's life all about?" Our life hinges on these two questions— the most important questions that any human being can ask. Somehow we know that our personal happiness depends on finding the answers—that if we only knew what life was really about, then we would have the roadmap to fulfillment in our lives. That's why we have a natural inclination to search. However, we often search in all the wrong places. We can go the way of Mr. Potter or the way of George Bailey.

People have been asking "Who am I?" and "What's life all about?" ever since Adam and Eve. Saint John Paul II said that the Book of Genesis describes man as one standing before God in search of his own identity (TOB 5:5). Because so many people before you have wrestled with these questions, you can benefit from their hard work. Of all the great thinkers, however, Aristotle said it best.

THE WAY TO TRUE HAPPINESS

Aristotle was a famous ancient Greek philosopher who lived about 2,500 years ago. He was a student of Plato, who was a student of Socrates. In his work *Nicomachean Ethics*, Aristotle said that the meaning of life is to be happy, and that ultimately happiness is the thing that everybody is searching for. However, Aristotle meant something very specific by happiness. For Aristotle, "happiness" means "fulfillment." Understood this way, happiness refers to

> **WORD TO THE WISE**
>
> The word Aristotle used for happiness, *eudemonia*, translates more literally as "fulfillment."

an internal condition that is the opposite of *emptiness*, not the opposite of sadness, suffering, or pain as many might think. Happiness is a deep sense of peace and contentment in one's soul. And it can actually *co-exist* with sadness, suffering, and pain. Your world could be falling apart and you could be enduring great trials, yet you would still be able to feel content and peaceful in your heart because you are *fulfilled.* True happiness, therefore, doesn't come and go; it is enduring. And this is precisely the happiness that everybody longs for. Those who say things like, "I'll only be happy if I get that car, go to that college, or get that girlfriend or boyfriend," or "I'll only be happy if my lousy circumstances change," sadly don't understand what true happiness is and are only setting themselves up to be disappointed. True happiness happens from the inside out, not the outside in. This is why Aristotle said that there are three main ways in which people tend to seek happiness. Mr. Potter exemplifies the first two, and George Bailey the third.

Notable Quotable

Virtuous activities and their opposites are what constitute happiness or the reverse.

—Aristotle

The first is the way of pleasure. This way promises fulfillment by pleasing the senses and avoiding pain at all costs. It involves lots of eating, drinking, and sex; always looking toward the new and improved "high." It looks no farther than the next party. Aristotle called those who seek fulfillment in this way "vulgar" and "animalistic." He wasn't trying to be mean—he was simply stating that those who live this life lower themselves to the level of animals. Aristotle concluded that such people will never find the fulfillment they seek. If you look at people who seem to have all the pleasure they want, yet still seem unhappy and empty inside, you'll see Aristotle was right.

The second is the way of power. This way promises fulfillment from being popular and having many possessions. It's all about stardom and stuff. In the eyes of the world, these things make a person powerful. They unlock the door to all the fine food and drink, drugs, sex, and material possessions that one could possibly imagine. In this sense, the life of power merely provides the means to the life of pleasure. Like those who seek the life of pleasure, those who seek the life of power don't find the fulfillment they seek either. Popularity evaporates, here one minute and gone the next. It depends on others' opinions of you, after all, and you can't control that. Money can run out; the stock market can crash; thieves can "break in and steal." What then?

The third is the way of virtue. This way promises fulfillment from living a morally good life. The word *virtue* comes from the Latin word *vir*, meaning "man." So, virtue literally means "manliness" or "humanliness." Virtue is human perfection. *Being virtuous means being excellent at being human.* Think about those we honor in history as great people, as opposed to those we revile as scoundrels. Isn't virtue the criterion? We call them great people because they represent the best that humans have to offer, because they exemplify everything we aspire to be.

So, what was Aristotle's conclusion? *Human fulfillment results from being fully human.* If you want to be happy, then you've got to be human. Only then will you be truly rich.

Now, you may ask: What does it really mean to be human? *The first lesson that Jesus teaches us from* The Cosmic Prequel *answers this great question.* Jesus knows that we can't even begin to understand what human love, human sexuality, marriage, and family life are all about—let alone find fulfillment in them—until we first understand what being human is all about.

Let's go back to the beginning with Jesus and discover what God had in mind when he created us. The key to a rich life is just around the corner!

JOHN PAUL II
In His Own Words

Happiness is being rooted in Love.

(TOB 16:2)

THINGS TO PONDER AND SHARE

1. Look at your life and the world around you. Do you know someone like George Bailey?

2. If you were asked to give your "Life Motto"—a phrase that sums up who you are and what your life is about—what would it be and why?

3. How did Aristotle understand happiness? How do many people today understand it? What's the difference?

4. According to Aristotle, what are the three different types of lives that humans can lead to try to find fulfillment? What was his conclusion? Do you agree? Why or why not?

5. When have you pursued happiness in pleasure, popularity, or possessions? How did it turn out in the short term? In the long term?

6. Who do you think are the great human beings in our world's history? What made them great?

·· READ THE CATECHISM OF THE CATHOLIC CHURCH ·····

nos. 27, 1718, 1723, 1803

CHAPTER 3

A STRIKING SIMILARITY

Then God said, "Let us make man in our image, after our likeness; and let them have dominion over the fish of the sea, and over the birds of the air, and over the cattle, and over all the earth, and over every creeping thing that creeps upon the earth." So God created man in his own image, in the image of God he created him; male and female he created them. And God blessed them, and God said to them, "Be fruitful and multiply, and fill the earth and subdue it; and have dominion over the fish of the sea and over the birds of the air and over every living thing that moves upon the earth."

Did U Know

The word "man" can refer to a male human being or to humanity as a whole—both men and women. The latter is how it is intended here. This is important to keep in mind as you read quotes from Scripture or from Saint John Paul II.

—Genesis 1:26–28

CREATED IN THE IMAGE AND LIKENESS OF GOD

One of my favorite books when I was a small boy was *Are You My Mother?* by P. D. Eastman. Maybe you've read it. It's a story about a little bird that hatches while his mother is away from the nest gathering food. When he breaks out of his egg, his first instinct is to identify his mother. Realizing that she is not there, he decides to go looking for her. But since he doesn't know what his mother looks like, he travels from creature to creature and thing to thing asking the question: Are you my mother? The book then recounts the perilous adventures of this poor little bird as he searches for his mommy.

For whatever reason, this book reached into my heart when I was a little boy. Maybe I felt as though I could identify with this little bird, since I had gotten lost my share of times in the local department store and had felt that hole in the pit of my stomach as I frantically looked for my parents up and down every aisle. Or maybe it was simply because I had a deep sense of compassion for him. After all, the little bird was all alone, separated from his mother, and since he didn't know where he came from, he had no idea what he was. Talk about an identity crisis!

The climactic event of the story comes when the little guy meets the "Snort," which is really a huge construction crane, and it unexpectedly places him back into his nest. At that very moment, the mother bird returns. She asks her little one, "Do you know who I am?" The birdie replies, "You are not a kitten. You are not a hen. You are not a dog. You are not a cow. You are not a boat, or a plane, or a Snort! You are a bird, and you are my mother." And the two presumably live happily ever after.

Well, believe it or not, we have a lot in common with that little bird. The truth is that if we are going to know who we are as human beings, we are first going to have to know where we come from. And that's exactly why the first passage that Jesus refers to in his response to the Pharisees' question about divorce is the creation story of Genesis 1.

This passage makes it resoundingly clear that we come from God and that we are created in *his image and likeness*. Now, of course, to be made in God's image and likeness doesn't mean to be God himself. As creatures, we are much more *unlike* God than like him. Yet, the revelation that we are made in the image of God gives us the key to unlocking the meaning and purpose of our existence. If we could know *who God is*, then we could discover *who we are*. So, based on what the Scriptures tell us about who God is, what do we learn about who we are as creatures made in God's image and likeness?

PERSONS WHO CAN THINK AND CHOOSE

First, we can see that God is a thinking-choosing sort of being. Notice in the passage how deliberately he chooses to create the world, especially human beings: "Let us make man in our image, after our likeness; and let them have dominion over the fish of the sea, and over the birds of the air, and over the cattle, and over all the earth, and over every creeping thing that creeps upon the earth" (Gen 1:26). It's also striking that God is clearly a rational being. He has thought through exactly what he is going to do, and then he does it.

Thus, the first thing it means to be made in the image of God is that, like God, *each of us is a thinking-choosing sort of being.* And we have a name we give to thinking-choosing beings: we call them *persons*. Persons can think and choose, precisely because they have the "powers" to do so; that is, they have *intellects* and they have *wills*. These powers give them some unique capacities. For one, they are the only beings that are *free* or "in charge" of themselves. That means that persons alone are capable of determining who they are and who they will become by their own free choices. In addition, since persons are *free* or "in charge" of themselves, they are the only beings that can truly *give* themselves to another person or persons. This is because gifts, by their very nature, must always be free.

NOTABLE QUOTABLE

Man . . . cannot fully find himself except through a sincere gift of himself.

—*Pastoral Constitution on the Church in the Modern World,* no. 24

However, an important point should be mentioned here. A person is not a person just because he or she is actually able to use these powers and capacities.

Instead, someone is a person because he or she is the *sort of being* that has these powers and capacities. This is a crucial distinction. Otherwise, we would have to say that infants and those with certain disabilities aren't persons at all, which of course is absurd.

Because persons have intellects and wills, are free and "in charge" of themselves, and can give themselves to another person or persons, they are also capable of love. In fact, the very reason persons have these powers and capacities is *so* they can love. And this leads to the second thing it means to be made in the image of God: *we were made to love as God loves.*

MADE FOR TRUE LOVE

In the Scriptures, whenever we find the word "love" referring to God, it's always a certain kind of love: a love traditionally called *charity.* You could say that charity is "God's brand" of love. This means that charity is the "true love" we were made for! But how might someone define this kind of love? I believe that Saint John Paul II would say that love is *the sincere gift of self.* Since this point is so important, let's break down this definition piece by piece.

"Sincere"—This means that love must be *genuine.* It has to really be about the other person and what is good for them. It cannot be a disguise for selfishness or for using or manipulating someone for your own purposes. This is a key point because selfishness and use often masquerade as love, but they aren't love at all. To be

"sincere," love must also be *true*. Saint Paul said that love "does not rejoice over wrongdoing but rejoices with the truth" (1 Cor 13:6). In other words, love is about what is *truly good* for the other person. And what is good is not a matter of opinion or personal feelings, but is rather something *objectively true* that is *known* by the *intellect*. You can't have "true love" without knowing "the truth" about what is good.

"*Gift*"— This means that love is something *freely given*, that is, something *chosen* or *willed*. A gift can only be a gift if it is free. This means that love is primarily a decision we make, not a feeling or an emotion. This is not to say that love is emotion*less* or that there is no such thing as a feeling of love. Such emotions and feelings are very real and rooted in human nature. It's just to say that real love is in the choosing, not in the feeling. Actually, sometimes choosing what is good doesn't feel good at all. In fact, it can entail great suffering—like enduring the ridicule of your peers because you stand up for the kid who is being picked on. And this leads to another point: since love is a gift, that also means it costs something. Love involves *sacrifice*. The greatness of the love is determined by the willingness to sacrifice, which is nothing other than the amount one is willing to give of him or herself. That's what makes Jesus' love so amazing (see Jn 15:13 and Rom 5:8). It is a love that empties itself completely for the one loved. Love isn't as much about giving some*thing* as it is about giving some*one*! You may not think that you are giving yourself to your parents when you're washing the dishes or taking out the garbage, but, assuming that you are doing it willingly, that is exactly what you are doing.

FEATURES OF TRUE LOVE

Now, this "true love" we have described also has certain features, especially as it is lived out in our everyday lives. These features are summed up beautifully in Saint Paul's great ode to love in his first letter to the Corinthians:

> *Love is patient and kind; love is not jealous or boastful; it is not arrogant or rude. Love does not insist on its own way; it is not irritable or resentful; it does not rejoice at wrong, but rejoices in the right. Love bears all things, believes all things, hopes all things, endures all things. (1 Cor 13:4–7)*

Pope Francis offers a lovely meditation on this passage in his work *The Joy of Love*, which can also serve as an "examination of conscience" that helps us to see those areas where we love well and those where we could love better. *Patience* does not mean being passive or allowing ourselves to be mistreated, but thinking before we speak or act. This will help us avoid words or actions that are hurtful so that we don't do anything we will only regret later. *Kindness* is about noticing and caring for the needs of others. *Not being jealous* means that love is concerned with the happiness of others and values their personal achievements. *Not being boastful* means being focused on others and not only on ourselves, for love is not "puffed up," but "builds up." *Not being rude* means avoiding harshness in the way we

speak or act toward others, and trying to avoid con-
flicts when possible. *Not seeking its own interests* does
not mean that we shouldn't love ourselves, but that we
should be generous in our giving, expect nothing in
return, and seek *to love* more than *to be loved*. *Not
being irritable or resentful* means we should not nur-
ture interior hostility or irritation, for this only causes
us to view others cynically or with contempt. *Not rejoicing in wrongdoing* can mean "takes no account of evil,"
and this emphasizes that *love forgives*, even when this
is very difficult to do. *Rejoicing in the right* means seeing and celebrating the good in others and the good
they do. *Bearing all things* not only refers to putting up
with evil, but has to do with "holding the tongue"—love
refuses to speak ill of others, tries to present them in
the best possible light, and resists the tendency to try
to make ourselves look good by highlighting someone
else's faults. *Believes all things* means that love trusts;
hopes all things means that love is convinced that people can change and grow; *endures all things* means
that love not only bears trials or tolerates annoyances,
but never gives up. Love is always ready to confront
challenges, even when things seem bleak.

All of these features of "true love" are ways we can
give the sincere gift of ourselves each and every day.
They teach us how to love as God loves in the ordinary
and extraordinary situations in life. They all point to
the truth that love is focused on the good of others and
demands that we purify ourselves of our tendency to
self-centeredness.

GETTING CONNECTED: MADE FOR COMMUNION

When persons give the sincere gift of themselves to one another, they become *spiritually united* or "connected" with one another; that is, they form what is called a *communion of persons.* A communion of persons is a relationship of "mutual gift" in which each person affirms and confirms the inherent value of the other, in effect saying, "I am *for you* and want what is best for you." And this leads to the third thing it means to be made in the image of God: *we were made for a communion of persons.* You could say that to be human means to "get connected."

It is the Christian belief that God himself is a communion of persons! This is what the doctrine of the Holy Trinity is all about. God is *three Persons*—the Father, the Son, and the Holy Spirit—*in one God.* God is three distinct Persons who share a common nature, and are completely one with each other because of their mutual love. The Father loves the Son from all eternity. He gives himself fully to his Son because he loves the Son fully. The Son receives and accepts the love and gift of the Father. He returns the Father's total self-giving with his own and gives himself fully to the Father because he loves the Father fully. Since the gift that is given from the Father to the Son and from the Son to the Father *is God* (the total self-gift of God would necessarily be God), then the Gift itself, the Love between the Father and the Son, is another Divine Person. We call that Person the Holy Spirit.

It is easy to see, therefore, what Saint John meant when he wrote those famous words, "God is love" (1 Jn 4:8). God's very nature is love as a self-giving communion of persons. But this also means that, in God, love and life are synonyms! God is love (1 Jn 4:8) and God is life (Jn 14:6). The Father's love (his gift of self) begets the Son, and from the love of the Father and the Son (the total gift of the Father and the Son to one another) the Spirit of Love proceeds. And, out of love, the life-giving communion of Persons we call the Trinity created the universe!

> **COMING ATTRACTIONS**
>
> As we will see later on, the most fundamental example of a life-giving communion of persons is marriage and the family.

So, being made in the image of the Trinity means that we are made for a life-giving communion of persons too! In fact, this is the ultimate way in which we image God, because it is the whole point of being persons who can give the sincere gift of themselves. In this, human beings find the meaning of their being and existence. They find true happiness.

With all of this said, here is a good description of who human beings are and what the meaning of human life is:

Human beings, as persons created
in the image of God, are endowed with intellects
and wills, so they can make the sincere gift of
themselves to one another and form a communion of
persons, and thereby finding true happiness.

FOR YOUR CONSIDERATION

Brackets in a quote mean that the words are mine and are used to clarify a speaker's identity or to make a word or phrase more understandable.

You could say that we bear a striking similarity to God. Yet, although God and we are similar in that we are persons who are oriented toward love and communion, God is pure spirit (as are the angels) and we aren't. We have bodies. God made us "body-persons," who are both matter and spirit. And this is what makes us one of a kind in all creation!

JOHN PAUL II
In His Own Words

From the beginning" [man is] . . . essentially the image of an inscrutable divine communion of Persons.

(TOB 9:3)

This same man, willed in this way by the Creator from the "beginning," can only find himself through a disinterested gift of self.

(TOB 15:3)

THINGS TO PONDER AND SHARE

1. Think of a time in your life when you faced an "identity crisis"—when you seriously questioned who you were or who you were becoming. How did you resolve it?

2. What are the three ways we bear a striking similarity to God? Briefly explain each.

3. What is a simple definition of love? Define the two parts of this simple definition: *sincere* and *gift*. How is this different from the way love is commonly understood?

4. What are some concrete ways you can give the sincere gift of yourself for the good of your parents? Your grandparents? Your brothers and sisters? Your friends? Your church? Your town? The poor, the lonely, or the unfairly treated?

5. Think about a time in your life when you gave or failed to give yourself for another person and their good without thought of return. What did you learn from that experience?

6. What does the phrase "communion of persons" mean? What are some examples of such "communions"?

·· READ THE CATECHISM OF THE CATHOLIC CHURCH ····

nos. 356–358, 1702–1705, 1766, 2331

CHAPTER 4

OUR BODIES ARE US!

[T]hen the LORD God formed man of dust from the ground, and breathed into his nostrils the breath of life; and man became a living being. And the LORD God planted a garden in Eden, in the east; and there he put the man whom he had formed.

— Genesis 2:7–8

BODY AND SOUL

A story is told about four people named Everybody, Somebody, Anybody, and Nobody. An important job had to be done and Everybody was sure that Somebody would do it. Anybody could have done it, but Nobody did it. Somebody got angry about that, because it was Everybody's job. Everybody thought Anybody could do it, but Nobody realized that Everybody wouldn't do it. It ended up that Everybody blamed Somebody when Nobody did what Anybody could have done.

What's my takeaway from this story about responsibility? *No* **body** is *any* **body**; *every* **body** is *somebody*. Remember how I mentioned at the end of the last chapter that human beings are body-persons? We have a soul with an intellect and will (which is what makes it possible for us to be *responsible* like the characters in the story), *and* we have a body with all its senses. Yet, the human body is not simply "any body," like some kind of generic material container for the soul. Every body (every human body anyway) reveals a "somebody," that is, a unique and unrepeatable person created in the image and likeness of God. And so, our bodies are us, and they are holy! This, in fact, is the next lesson Jesus wished to teach us by taking us back to "the beginning."

FOR YOUR CONSIDERATION

None of this means that these opening passages of the Bible must be taken literally as exact descriptions of historical events. That's not even how the people who wrote them understood them. These passages use mythical figures and images to describe primordial events and truths about God, us, and the world.

The second passage Jesus alludes to in his answer to the Pharisees is the creation story in Genesis 2 (the Book of Genesis has *two* creation stories). Even though Genesis 1 states that God created human beings "male and female," Genesis 2 gives us the specifics of *how* and *why* he did so. The passage begins with the creation of the first man, Adam, from the dust or clay of the ground. Although Adam gets his name from the stuff he is made of (*adamah* is the Hebrew word for "earth"), this doesn't mean that men are dirt. After God creates Adam from the clay of the ground, he breathes into him "the breath of life," and Adam becomes a "living being." The Hebrew word for "breath," *ruah*, is the same word for "spirit." So, the breath of life indicates that human beings are both physical *and* spiritual beings. In other words, they are *body-persons*. The sad reality is, however, that many people do not know this important truth.

DIFFERENT VIEWS OF THE BODY

One school of thought holds that a person is really identified with the soul, not the body. In other words, the soul is the real you. The body dies, after all, and the soul goes to heaven (or that other place). In this view, the body is like a prison for the soul and is always making us do bad things. You could classify these ideas as being "down" on the body.

Another view holds that the soul does not exist at all, that we are just matter, and that when we're dead, we're dead. Life is merely about gaining pleasure and avoiding pain. "Eat, drink, and be merry, for tomorrow we die" sums up this creed.

Both of these views are flawed. Catholicism holds that human beings are both body and soul, not more one than the other. The fact that we die and our souls separate from our bodies is not part of God's original plan for us. Though death is natural for beings with bodies, in "the beginning" God gave human beings the gift of immortality so that their bodies took on the immortal quality of their souls. They kept this gift as long as their souls cleaved to God. So, you could say that God would "hold them together" as long as they "held onto him." For human beings, therefore, death is a consequence of Original Sin (more on that later).

PROOFS OF THE GOODNESS OF THE BODY

Jesus gives us proof positive of the body's goodness as an essential part of human beings. If the body were bad, the Son of God would have never become enfleshed, and he certainly would not have taken his body back after he died. Not only that, Jesus ascended into heaven body and soul. And check this one out: after his resurrection he even ate (see Jn 21:12–14)! If that wasn't enough, the Blessed Virgin Mary was assumed into heaven body and soul. After she died, God took her right up!

Catholics believe in what we call "the resurrection of the body": at the end of time, we will all get our bodies back. They will be new and different from the ones we have now—what the Scriptures refer to as "spiritual bodies." We will go to heaven (or that other place) with our body and our soul, for all eternity (see Jn 5:25–29). In heaven we will not have an out-of-body experience, but a "body-soul" experience! We will not just feel peace and fulfillment in our souls, but also experience the most radical bodily pleasure ever imagined. The Scriptures indicate that there will be "a new heaven and a new earth" (Rev 21:1, 2 Pet 3:13) in which Christ will make all things new (see Rev 21:5). Our faith teaches us that, at the end of time, the visible universe will be transformed and renewed, that the material universe and we share a profound common destiny (see *CCC* 1042, 1043, 1046, 1047). While we do not know exactly what heaven will be like, and any images we use will remain speculative and fall tremendously short of the reality, I think that heaven will be both familiar and yet beyond what our eyes have seen, or ears have heard, or minds have imagined (see 1 Cor 2:9). In God, we will rediscover all that was true, good, and beautiful in our earthly lives but in its perfection, and thus it will all seem brand new to us. I personally believe that heaven will have colorful sunsets, fragrant flowers, delicious food, and awesome music beyond what anyone has ever dreamed, as well as thrilling ski slopes and competitive baseball games. And of course, my family and friends will be there to enjoy it all with me. This is all pretty awesome news, unless, of course, you wind up going to that other place. I'll leave that to your imagination. Let's just say that it will be as wretched as heaven is beautiful.

God said that the physical world is "very good" (Gen 1:31), and therefore the experiences of the body are also very good. Jesus himself loved good food and good drink and even wondered if people would call him a glutton and a drunkard for it (see Mt 11:18–19)! I'm sure I don't have to convince you that he obviously was neither.

Since the physical world is good and the body is essential to being human, Catholicism emphasizes the important role of the senses in human life, as well as in our relationship with God. God comes to us through the physical world and through our seeing, smelling, hearing, tasting, and touching. Just think about the Bible: burning bushes, pillars of cloud and fire, Passover meals, etc. Of course, there's Jesus himself, the "image of the invisible God" (Col 1:15). He was *God made man*— talk about God coming to us through the physical world! Also, think about the sacraments that Jesus instituted as a way for us to reach out and touch the divine—water, oil, bread, wine, the spoken word, bodily actions. This is all pretty earthy stuff. That's because Jesus knew that we are body-persons, and that he needs to come to us through our senses.

THE BODY REVEALS THE PERSON

Now, just because we are equally body and soul doesn't mean that they are equal players. The soul is supposed to be "in charge of" or, in traditional language, "move" the body. And even *within* the soul there is a certain hierarchy or ordering of powers. The intellect is supposed to be in charge of or move the will. So, the way God originally intended us to work from "the beginning" is as follows: the intellect knows what is good, and the will, acting in and through the body, chooses that good. This means that the body and the soul stand or fall together.

It also means that the body *reveals* the person. It is in and through the body that the person, a being with an intellect and will, is made visible and is able to be perceived and experienced. We *are* our bodies, though we *are not merely* our bodies. Thus, how we treat our body is how we treat ourselves. How we look at or treat another's body is how we look at or treat her or him. And when we give our bodies, we give ourselves.

Since all human beings are created to love as God loves and give themselves as gifts to one another (in a way similar to but not exactly like the way husbands and wives love each other), the

NOTABLE QUOTABLE

It is neither the spirit alone nor the body alone that loves: it is man, the person, a unified creature composed of body and soul, who loves. Only when both dimensions are truly united, does man attain his full stature.

—Pope Benedict XVI

human body has what Saint John Paul II called a "spousal meaning." This means that *the body has the capacity to express the kind of love in which a person becomes a gift*. In fact, this is what God created the human body for. It is in and through the body that human beings give the sincere gift of themselves and make visible God's own self-giving love in the world.

Saint John Paul II strongly believed that these truths are essential to understanding the meaning and purpose of our existence. Because the body reveals the person and has a spousal meaning, human beings are not merely made in the image of God, but are *the physical image of God* in the world!

So, let's refine our earlier description of human beings and the meaning of life:

*Human beings, as body-persons created
in the image of the Trinity, are endowed
with intellects, wills, and bodies in order to be
the physical image of God in the world by making
the sincere gift of themselves to one another
in and through their bodies and forming a communion
of persons, thereby finding true happiness.*

Now we're getting somewhere.

JOHN PAUL II
In His Own Words

The human body, with its sex—its masculinity and femininity—seen in the very mystery of creation, is not only a source of fruitfulness and of procreation, as in the whole natural order, but contains "from the beginning" the "spousal" attribute, that is *the power to express love: precisely that love in which the human person becomes a gift* and—through this gift—fulfills the very meaning of his being and existence.

(TOB 15:1)

THINGS TO PONDER AND SHARE

1. What are some ways in which people can "undervalue" the body? What are some ways they can "overvalue" the body?

2. Define *adamah* and *ruah*. What do they reveal to us about man?

3. From your experience of church, give some examples of how Catholicism emphasizes the importance of the senses in human life.

4. What does it mean that the body "reveals the person" and has a "spousal meaning"? Why are these truths essential to understanding the meaning and purpose of our existence?

5. How should the fact that "the body reveals the person" affect the way we treat our body or other people's bodies? Give some concrete examples.

6. Reflecting on the quote from Saint John Paul II in the "In His Own Words" section, give some examples of the body's "spousal meaning" in action.

··READ THE CATECHISM OF THE CATHOLIC CHURCH ····

nos. 362–368, 1015–1017, 1146

CHAPTER 5

LESSONS IN LONELINESS

Then the LORD God said, "It is not good that the man should be alone; I will make him a helper fit for him." So out of the ground the LORD God formed every beast of the field and every bird of the air, and brought them to the man to see what he would call them; and whatever the man called every living creature, that was its name. The man gave names to all cattle, and to the birds of the air, and to every beast of the field; but for the man there was not found a helper fit for him.

—Genesis 2:18–20

WHY GOD MADE ADAM ALONE

While I'm not that bad at math in general, algebra was definitely not my subject. No matter how many different ways my teacher explained things, I just didn't get it. So on those occasions when I felt particularly lost, I would seek out the help of a tutor. The intense, individual attention really helped me to fully and properly understand the lessons being taught to me. I am convinced that without it, I'd still be in the tenth grade.

As a body-person, Adam in the earlier passage from Genesis has been made to love as God loves: to give the sincere gift of himself for the good of another through his body. No other creature has been made this way, and Adam knows it. But there's one small problem . . . there is no "other" to love. At least, not yet. For the time being, God wants Adam to be alone. God needs to teach him some important lessons, and unless Adam is alone, he won't fully and properly understand them. You could say that God scheduled some one-on-one tutoring in order to guarantee "educational success."

THE FIRST LESSON: BESIDES GOD THERE IS NO OTHER

Now, your first thought may be: "But isn't there God? Isn't he an 'other'? Isn't he the 'ultimate other'?" That is an excellent point! In fact, it's the first reason why God made Adam with no "other" to love. He wanted Adam to realize that besides him *there is no other. He* had to be first in Adam's life.

God is the *Alpha* and *Omega* (Rev 1:8), the beginning and the end—and everything in between. We owe our life and all that's in it to him. He made us, after all; we belong to him. He holds us in existence. He is everything, and without him we would be nothing. As a result, we should love him above all things. This is the first lesson that God wants to teach Adam in his "loneliness." Adam has more lessons to learn, however.

THE SECOND LESSON: LOVE REQUIRES KNOWING WHAT IS GOOD

God wanted to make it absolutely clear to Adam that love must be sincere and therefore about what is really good for a person, so he decided it was time to teach Adam about what is good and what is evil. Remember the tree? The one that Adam couldn't eat from without dying? God had a good reason to call it the tree of the knowledge of good and evil. When God forbids Adam from eating of the fruit of this tree, lesson number two begins.

COMING ATTRACTIONS

In chapter 9, I deal with the question of why Adam would "surely die" if he were to "make his own rules."

Look at the tree in this way: "not eating of the tree" means "choosing what God decides is good and not choosing what God decides is evil." On the other hand, "eating of the tree" means "deciding for yourself what is good and what is evil." Sound familiar? It is the quintessential clash within our culture and within ourselves: absolute truth vs. moral relativism, God's way vs. our way.

Moral relativism states that moral truth is *relative* to the individual: "Right and wrong is whatever you decide it is." People who ascribe to this view usually think that moral truths do not really exist, or at least that we cannot know what they are. They may also hold that morality is relative to culture and is merely a social convention. On the contrary, absolute truth means that moral truth is objective and universal: "There is a right and wrong, and it is right and wrong always, everywhere, and for everybody." It flows from the convictions that moral truth is something "given," something reasonable and knowable, and that God built fundamental laws that govern human behavior into the world he created. You could say that, in a way, every human choice places us at the tree. We always face the same temptation. Will we play by God's rules or try to make our own? Or will we even acknowledge that any rules exist at all?

If Adam is going to be an "image of God" and "love as God loves," then he needs to know *the truth* about *what is good*. You can't have love without truth. This is what many people today have sadly missed: if there is no absolute truth, there is no true love either. God's lesson to Adam is simple: if you are going to love, you must keep my commands (see Jn 14:15).

NOTABLE QUOTABLE

With this imagery [of the tree of the knowledge of good and evil], Revelation teaches that *the power to decide what is good and what is evil does not belong to man, but to God alone*. . . . God, who alone is good, knows perfectly what is good for man, and by virtue of his very love proposes this good to man in the commandments.

—Saint John Paul II

THE THIRD LESSON: PERSONS ARE DIFFERENT FROM ANIMALS

Next, God wanted Adam to really experience in the depths of his being that he was "alone" in the world; that he alone was a person capable of giving himself to another. Why would God want such a thing? Because it was the most powerful way for Adam to realize the purpose of his existence. When God declared, "It is not good that the man should be alone; I will make him a helper fit for him" (Gen 2:18), you can just imagine Adam's anticipation. Then, when the big moment finally arrived, the helper God created was . . . Eve, did you say? Nope. Actually, it was a cow. What a letdown!

Now, if you want to get technical, the Bible mentions both cows and birds by name, and then just states "and every beast of the field." But you must admit, God wasn't looking so bright just then. What was he doing? A *cow*? A *bird*? I mean, he has an omniscient reputation to live up to. You can almost see Adam's face saying, "You're kidding, right?"

Just a little tidbit: whenever God looks "dumb" in the Scriptures, it's obviously not that he *is* dumb, but that he's *playing* dumb. Why would he be playing dumb? Because God is a master teacher. Teachers typically ask their students loads of questions they already know the answers to. They do so because students learn better by coming to the answers themselves. Teachers play dumb; students get smart. That's what God was doing here.

So what was God teaching Adam in this final "lesson in loneliness"? Simply put: *you are not an animal.*

It's like God was saying, "Animals have bodies, but they aren't body-persons like you are. Animals know some things, but they don't know what is true, good, and beautiful like you do. Animals make some choices, but they're based on instinct or training, not on free choice like yours are. Animals may form an attachment to you and you may really care for them, but you can't love each other—at least not the way I love my Son or I love you. Let's face it, Adam, you can't form a communion of persons with a cow or a bird. No, you need an 'other' like yourself, whom you can love in and through your body!" Saint John Paul states that, in emphasizing how human beings are created in the image of God, the opening chapters of Genesis make clear that human beings cannot be reduced to or be fully explained in categories taken from the natural world (see TOB, 2:4).

Let's just say that Adam got the point. The more creatures he saw, the more alone he felt. Adam longed in the depths of his being for another whom he could love. Through the lessons he had learned in his loneliness, it became extremely clear to him that he would only find happiness and fulfill the purpose of existence by giving himself away to someone "just like him." This was Adam's deepest desire, and just when he thought all was lost, God met that desire . . . and then some.

JOHN PAUL II
In His Own Words

When God-Yahweh says, "It is not good that the man should be alone" (Gen 2:18), he affirms that, "alone," the man does not completely realize this essence [of being a person]. He realizes it only by existing *"with someone"*—and, put even more deeply and completely, by existing *"for someone."*

(TOB 14:2)

THINGS TO PONDER AND SHARE

1. Some of life's most memorable lessons are learned one-on-one. Recall a time in your life when a parent, a relative, a teacher, a coach, or some other caring adult or good friend pulled you aside and imparted wisdom to you.

2. List and explain the three lessons God taught Adam.

3. Have you ever put other people or things before God in your life? If so, when?

4. Why is obedience to God's commandments necessary in order to love?

5. Name a time in your life when you "made your own rules" instead of obeying God's rules. What were the results/consequences of that decision?

6. Define moral relativism. Give some examples of how moral relativism has become prevalent in our society.

7. How are humans different from animals?

·· READ THE CATECHISM OF THE CATHOLIC CHURCH ····

nos. 144, 299–301, 338, 342–343, 1955, 2465

CHAPTER 6

A MATCH MADE IN HEAVEN

So the LORD God caused a deep sleep to fall upon the man, and while he slept took one of his ribs and closed up its place with flesh; and the rib which the LORD God had taken from the man he made into a woman and brought her to the man. Then the man said, "This at last is bone of my bones and flesh of my flesh; she shall be called Woman, because she was taken out of Man." Therefore a man leaves his father and his mother and cleaves to his wife, and they become one flesh. And the man and his wife were both naked, and were not ashamed.

—Genesis 2:21–25

THE CREATION OF EVE AND THE FIRST MARRIED COUPLE

It's nearly impossible to listen to the radio, watch TV, or go online without being barraged by ads for some "matchmaking" service. Countless companies out there are trying to convince people that they have the fool-proof system for finding their "perfect match" and the man or woman of their dreams. No doubt these services can be helpful for some people, and I know couples who have gotten married after meeting through one of them. That being said, the Book of Genesis dramatically reveals that God is the "Supreme Matchmaker" and *the One who will make our dreams of real love come true*!

God puts Adam into a deep sleep, takes one of his ribs, and creates the helper of his dreams. Talk about a match made in heaven! After Adam awakes, his delight could probably be heard from a mile away. "Wow!" he exclaims. "She's beautiful. She's perfect. She's my equal. She's just like me . . . but different in all the right ways! We belong together! At last, one whom I can love in and through my body; one for whom I can give my life!" I truly believe that this is the gist of the whole "bone of my bones and flesh of my flesh" thing.

You see, God didn't really make Eve "just like" Adam. He made her a person like Adam, but he made her very different from Adam. God made Eve *complementary* to Adam. We know this because she was made to be his "helper." God knew all along that he was going to make them *to be each other's helpers*.

Think about when you typically ask for help. Isn't it usually when you can't do something? A helper is someone who makes up for what you lack. A helper is someone whose gifts complement your own. When people help each other, they are more together than they are individually.

This is why God made human beings male and female. He made man with "a guy way of thinking, being, and acting" called *masculinity*, and he made woman with "a girl way of thinking, being, and acting" called *femininity*. While this has been misunderstood and used to perpetuate gender stereotypes or even social injustice, it is important to acknowledge that masculinity and femininity are real and not exclusively socially constructed. The differences between men and women are an essential and important part of our humanity and our human relationships and are vital to a well-functioning society. Masculinity and femininity are harmonious. Man and woman are equal in dignity because they are both persons made in the image of God. But God created them differently so each could make their own special and unique gift of themselves. A man cannot make a woman's gift, and a woman cannot make a man's gift. This makes their union melodious rather than monotone, a symphony rather than a solo. And men and women each have notes in this symphony that only they can play. I don't know about you, but it is music to my ears!

In addition, God created men and women with complementary bodies. The first man and woman understood that their bodies were made for union with each other and had a *spousal* or *unitive* meaning, that is, the capacity of expressing love and communion. After the birth of the first child, they also learned that their bodies had a *procreative* or *generative* meaning, that is, that their bodies were made to give life and participate in the mystery of creation (see Gen 4:1). The unitive and procreative meanings of the body were stamped by God right into its very structure. The first human couple perceived this clearly.

Yet today it can seem as if some in our culture do not clearly perceive the truth that we are created by God as male or female, and that this corresponds to the biological sex with which we are born. Some even reject this truth. Pope Francis has stated strongly that the Church cannot accept a "gender ideology" that proposes that people should be able to "identify" as male, female, in-between, neither, or both, regardless of their biological sex. Such an ideology would not only deny the creation of human beings as male and female in the image of God, but would deny the inherent complementarity of man and woman and the truth about the human body.

This said, we are becoming more aware of people who experience difficulties coming to terms with their creation by God as male or female. This is often very confusing for them and can be the source of great suffering. If you are experiencing such challenges it is important for you to hear that God loves you and that you are wonderful to him. The Lord is with you in your struggle. And so is the Church.

Pope Francis has said that when we encounter people who are struggling in this way, we should do what Jesus would do: we should welcome them, try to understand what they are going through, accompany them, and seek to draw them into the life of the community. As Christians we should make visible the love and compassion of Jesus in the way we interact with and speak about our brothers and sisters who are trying to understand themselves and their feelings. If we fail to do this, they may choose to walk away from the Church and turn elsewhere in a search for acceptance, even to a place that reinforces false ideas about how to understand their struggle. But only Jesus offers the truth that will set us free and can give our hearts the love and acceptance we each truly seek!

GIVING THE BODY, GIVING THE SELF

Adam and Eve found what Saint John Paul II called "original happiness" in being each other's helper—in giving themselves for each other's true good. In biblical terms, Adam and Eve form a covenant with one another. In a covenant, people say to each other, "I am yours, and you are mine"; they make a solemn promise (known as a *vow*) in the presence of God to give themselves totally to each other and to become a family. Adam looked at Eve and said, "Eve, I give myself to you. I'm yours. And I will give myself for you and your true good

NOTABLE QUOTABLE

Marriage based on exclusive and definitive love becomes the icon of the relationship between God and his people and vice versa. God's way of loving becomes the measure of human love.

—Pope Benedict XVI

every day. I am your husband." Eve accepted Adam's gift and returned it with a gift of her own: "And I, Adam, give myself to you. I am yours. And I will give myself for you and your true good every day. I am your wife." In making these promises, Adam and Eve commit to loving each other as God loves, a love that embodies all the features that Saint Paul highlighted in his letter: "Love is patient and kind . . ." (1 Cor 13:4).

God blesses the union of Adam and Eve, and then they do with their bodies what their words said—they give *themselves* totally to one another by giving *their bodies* totally to one another in sexual union. The Bible says they become "one flesh." This union ratifies their covenant, embodies their vows, and consummates their marriage. (In fact, it is only after they become "one flesh" that the biblical text refers to them as "man and wife"—see Genesis 2:24–25.) This gift of their bodies in sexual union is sincere because they indeed have given themselves to one another through their promises. The result of this sincere gift of themselves through the gift of their bodies must have been the most profound experience of bodily and spiritual communion between a man and a woman ever on this side of eternity!

When Adam and Eve become one flesh through their sexual union, God binds them together in love with *his own love*: the Holy Spirit! This is why, as Jesus reminds the Pharisees, "what God has joined no human being must separate" or *can* separate. No one can divide what God has united. Just as the Holy Spirit unites the Father and the Son, and they can never be separated from one another, the Holy Spirit unites the husband and wife, and they can never be separated from one another. This is the *original unity* of man and woman as God intended it from "the beginning."

NOTABLE QUOTABLE

The Church continues to teach the unchanging truth that marriage is indissoluble. When couples freely receive this Sacrament [of Matrimony], they establish an unbreakable oneness. Their love for one another, their conjugal love, can last until death, not because of their own strength or merits but because of Christ's grace at work within them.

—Saint John Paul II

THE NAKED TRUTH

This verse brings to our attention another very "revealing" topic: *nakedness*. Why did God inspire the biblical author to note that Adam and Eve were "naked and not ashamed"? Two reasons stand out, and both tell us something about the human body and the way we look at it. First, Adam and Eve were not ashamed of their nakedness because they recognized quite naturally that the body reveals the person. When they saw each other's bodies, they saw each other's *persons*. They didn't just see bodies. Just seeing bodies is the root of lust. The reduction of persons to their bodies actually depersonalizes them. It treats them like animals. They become nothing more than objects to be used according to another's good pleasure, certainly not persons to be loved for their own sakes.

Because they were inclined to *perceive the person*, Adam's "love handles" and the extra pounds around Eve's hips didn't embarrass them or make them ashamed. Our contemporary culture, with its obsession with six-pack abs and thigh gaps, has tragically missed this point. When Adam and Eve looked upon each other, all they saw was the most beautiful *person* in the entire world!

In order to understand the second reason why Adam and Eve were not ashamed of their nakedness, we need to interpret nakedness in a broader sense. To be naked can mean to be "exposed" or "vulnerable," "baring all" so to speak. Adam and Eve were completely open with each other, sharing everything: their thoughts, feelings, hopes, dreams, and fears. They allowed themselves to be vulnerable with each other. This took profound trust—but they felt safe. They knew they were completely focused on each other's good, so they had no fear of being used or manipulated by the other. They also had the confidence that in sharing their hearts with one another, the other person wouldn't break their heart by walking away.

It was only after sin came on the scene that they needed to "cover up." Only then did they need to protect their bodies from the lustful gaze of the other. Only then did they need to protect their hearts from being broken by use, manipulation, dishonesty, abandonment, and betrayal.

For now, however, they had found marital bliss. They had finally "met their match."

JOHN PAUL II
In His Own Words

In this way, for the first time, the man (male) shows joy and even exultation, for which he had no reason before, due to the lack of a being similar to himself. Joy for the other human being, for the second "I," dominates in the words the man (male) speaks on seeing the woman (female). All this helps to establish the full meaning of original unity.

(TOB 8:4)

THINGS TO PONDER AND SHARE

1. Have you ever dreamed about your future spouse, your "match made in heaven"? What are his or her personal qualities? Why would he or she be your perfect match?

2. What are the different ways in which men and women are complementary? How have some aspects of contemporary society tried to downplay or even deny these God-given differences? On the other hand, how have these differences been misunderstood and used to perpetuate gender stereotypes or even social injustice?

3. Have you ever been a helper to another person (parents, friends, the poor)? How did it make you feel?

4. How do the marriage vows (e.g., "for better or worse," etc.) express the meaning of life and human existence (i.e., "to love as God loves")? Why is marriage necessarily "until death do us part"? Why does sexual union only "speak the truth" after the marriage vows have been exchanged?

5. What are the two reasons that God inspired the biblical author to note that Adam and Eve were "naked and not ashamed"?

6. Give examples of how our society often fails to "perceive the person" revealed in his or her body and instead sees humans as "just bodies."

··READ THE CATECHISM OF THE CATHOLIC CHURCH ····

nos. 371, 373, 1605, 2333–2335

CHAPTER 7

GOD IS PRO-LIFE!

*God blessed them, and God said to them, "Be fruitful
and multiply, and fill the earth and subdue it."*

—Genesis 1:28

THE CALL TO FRUITFULNESS IN MARRIAGE

An old rhyme goes: "First comes love, then comes
marriage, then comes baby in a baby carriage." Though
it doesn't always happen this way, this simple phrase
illustrates a fundamental truth about human love and
human sexuality.

Fertility was the original blessing that the Creator
bestowed upon the first married couple, and, as we'll
see, it has everything to do with the "two becoming
one flesh" and being made in the image of the Trinity.
But it was also a *mission* God gave to the husband and
wife (and to every married couple that would come after

them). Notice that the sentence "Be fruitful and multiply" is an *imperative*: it gives a command. Here God is making clear that fruitfulness is a responsibility that is "built into" the nature of marriage itself.

Now, God did not say that the man and his wife had to have sex twenty-four hours a day, seven days a week—after all, they had a garden to care for and cultivate (see Gen 2:15). He also didn't say that they had to have as many children as was "humanly conceivable." But it is clear that *marriage is about family*—being fruitful and multiplying, and doing so generously, wasn't optional in God's original plan for marriage, but at the heart of it. And this generosity toward life was to be a *source of blessing* for the married couple and their children!

MARRIAGE: A LIFE-GIVING COMMUNION OF PERSONS

So, *why* would God command fruitfulness? And *how* could God command fruitfulness? Let's answer the first question first.

We have already shown that man and woman are persons who are made to love as God loves, in and through their bodies. We have also shown that God's love is a fruitful love that gives life. This is why in addition to the body's *spousal* or *unitive meaning*, which is its capacity to express love and communion, it has a *procreative* or *generative meaning*, which is its capacity to give life. When man and woman love as God loves, in and through their bodies, they form a communion of persons; they become completely one with each other or "one flesh." They most fully realize this one flesh communion of persons when, through their sexual union, the twenty-three chromosomes of the man become one with the twenty-three chromosomes of the woman. The child is the crowning event of the communion of the spouses. You could even say that the child is the love of the spouses made a person—made a *third* person. Saint John Paul II even described the child as the "third" who springs from the communion of the man and woman, and as the one in whom the man and woman can recognize themselves (see TOB 21:4). The total gift of the spouses to one another opens itself up to the gift of the child. When I look at each of my own children I see my and my wife's love *personified* and revealed to us in a radically new way. I see our gift become a gift.

As we have previously said, human beings are created for a life-giving communion of persons in the image of the Trinity. This is why when God creates human beings in his image he creates them male and female and blesses them with fruitfulness, that is, he creates a married couple, a family. And so, marriage and the family are created in the image of the Trinity! The human "we" of the family finds its eternal pattern in the divine "We" of the Trinity.

GENEROSITY TOWARD LIFE AND ITS BLESSINGS

Just as God's love is life-giving, the love of the spouses, as the image of God's love in the world, should always be willing to give life to others. The prevailing attitudes of the spouses ought to be generosity toward new life—that there is always enough love to go around—and hospitality—that the child is a gift to be welcomed with open hearts and open arms. As Pope Francis highlights in *The Joy of Love:* "Children are a gift. Each one is unique and irreplaceable. . . . We love our children because they are children, not because they are beautiful, or look or think as we do, or embody our dreams. We love them because they are children. A child is a child" (no. 170).

Also, with more children, both parents and children have *more* opportunities to love. Let's face it, larger families have fewer options. If everyone and everything is going to be taken care of, everybody must do his or her part. In a sense, each family member must "take it for the team." The older members tend to the younger ones, the more able to the less able, and the healthy to the sick. Actually, in my family each older child is assigned as the helper for a younger child and assists them in brushing their teeth, getting them dressed, making their beds, and the like. And just as with a team, in the end everybody wins. The spouses not only give the sincere gift of themselves to one another, but together they give the sincere gift of themselves to their children. In turn, the children give the sincere gift of themselves to each other and to their parents. As a result, every member of the family learns "to love as God loves" more perfectly with each passing day. This is why Saint Teresa of Kolkata used to say, "Love begins at home," and why Saint John Paul II was fond of calling the family a "school of love."

And since we only "find ourselves" and our happiness in the "sincere gift of ourselves" (that is, in loving as God loves), you could also call the family a "school of happiness." Everyone gives, everyone receives, and everyone is blessed.

GOD IS THE LORD OF LIFE

That should answer *why* God commands fruitfulness; now let's look at the *how*. God can command it because he is the one in charge of it. When Eve gives birth to her firstborn son, she exclaims, "I have gotten a man with the help of the LORD" (Gen 4:1). God is the sovereign Lord of life. The Holy Spirit is the "Lord and Giver of life." Man and woman are called to cooperate in God's creating, and not to do anything deliberately to stop it. That's why we say God creates, but humans pro-create. God commands man and woman to be "pro" or "in favor of" his creating when he wills it and to place no obstacle in the way of it. Make no mistake about it: God is pro-life!

> Even when procreation is not possible, [marital] life does not for this reason lose its value. Physical sterility . . . can be for spouses the occasion for other important services . . . , for example, adoption, various forms of educational work, and assistance to other families and poor or handicapped children.
>
> —Saint John Paul II

It's important to make clear that a couple that is *naturally* infertile, who through no deliberate choice is physically unable to bear children, do not have "less" of a marriage than a couple who has been blessed with many children. Neither is this couple "cursed" by God or "judged" by him as not deserving of children. Disabilities and disorders in nature are part of life in a fallen world. Couples who desire children of their own, yet cannot conceive them, suffer tremendously. *A loving option for these couples is adoption.* Adopting children can help their love to grow in perfection as they include others in it, and allow them to more fully share in the Creator's original blessing.

Well, as we have seen, that original blessing means that God is pro-life. However, as Adam and Eve are about to learn, "The wages of sin is death" (Rom 6:23), not life.

JOHN PAUL II
In His Own Words

Procreation brings it about that "the man and the woman (his wife)" *know each other reciprocally [together] in the "third,"* originated by both. . . . [T]his "knowledge" becomes in some way a revelation of the new man, in whom both, the man and the woman, again recognize each other, their humanity, their living image.

(TOB 21:4)

1. What are some ways in which people mistakenly view children as a burden rather than a blessing?

2. How are marriage and the family created in the image of the Trinity as a life-giving communion of persons?

3. What is the procreative or generative meaning of the body?

4. Why would the Church support and encourage adoption, especially for naturally infertile couples?

5. How does the family help us to "love as God loves" every day? What are some families you know that are truly "schools of love"?

6. How is fruitfulness in marriage a blessing to both parents and children?

7. God is the sovereign Lord of life. What are some ways in which that is not acknowledged in our world today?

·· READ THE CATECHISM OF THE CATHOLIC CHURCH ····

nos. 372, 1604, 1652–1654

CHAPTER 8

GONE FISHING

Now the serpent was more subtle than any other wild creature that the LORD God had made. He said to the woman, "Did God say, 'You shall not eat of any tree of the garden'?" And the woman said to the serpent, "We may eat of the fruit of the trees of the garden; but God said, 'You shall not eat of the fruit of the tree which is in the midst of the garden, neither shall you touch it, lest you die.'" But the serpent said to the woman, "You will not die. For God knows that when you eat of it your eyes will be opened, and you will be like God, knowing good and evil."

—Genesis 3:1–5

THE FALL OF THE FIRST MAN AND WOMAN

I'm not a fisherman, but I went fishing once. A friend of mine was moving from New Jersey to Indiana, and he insisted on taking me fishing before he left. So we planned to go one morning. When I showed up at his house in the wee hours, he was all ready to go (he had even bought me my very own fishing pole). We drove to his favorite fishing hole, and he gave me a "crash course."

It turns out you need to know a few very important things to catch a fish. First, you've got to go where the fish are, that is, you've got to choose a good fishing hole. Second, you have to be as quiet and crafty as possible, so you don't scare the fish away. Third, you've got to choose the right bait: one that looks "good" or "harmless" to the fish, and can capture the fish's curiosity without alerting it to the danger. Finally, you need to cast a long line and reel it in slowly, so it looks natural and unassuming.

CHECK IT OUT

The serpent (Satan) turns up again at the end of the Scriptures.
See Revelation 12:9

Well, Satan, who is symbolically represented in Genesis 3 by the serpent, knows a thing or two about fishing. Adam and Eve . . . well, they're the fish. And, actually, so are we.

Try to imagine the scene. Still basking in the after-glow of marital bliss, Eve decides to go out for some breakfast. Adam follows, and the two of them stroll into the garden. It is a beautiful morning: the sun is shining on their faces, the birds are chirping, and a gentle breeze is blowing across the lightly dew-laden grass. The man and his wife sense within their souls the union they had formed with each other. They feel it really and truly—down to the core. They also feel a profound oneness with the world around them. Joy, peace, and harmony rule creation. You could say it is "heaven on earth." Many newlyweds experience something similar.

They are so caught up in the moment that they don't even realize they have meandered right into the middle of the garden. Then they see it: the tree. The serpent is already waiting. The tree is the "perfect fishing hole," and its fruit—the promise of *absolute freedom and independence*—the "perfect bait." Here Satan can try to get Adam and Eve to unlearn the lessons God had taught Adam in his loneliness: that they need God's rules in order to love and be truly happy, that besides God there is "no other," and that they are different from the animals. The serpent is ready to "cast a long line" in order to "hook" Adam and Eve. But he can't be obvious, lest he scare them away. He needs to be "subtle."

SATAN THE SPIN DOCTOR

In this case, to be subtle means to be crafty or cunning—to be a master of fine distinctions. It means being able to take words and give them a little twist, practically undetectable yet enough to affect their meaning. It essentially means being a "spin doctor." In Satan's case, it means being particularly adept at *making what's good look like it's evil, and what's evil look like it's good* in order to get us to believe that God didn't really mean what he said or that somehow there's an exception for us.

Here's a modern example of Satan whispering subtleties in our ears:

"You love each other, right? Then go ahead and have sex! Sex is about love after all. It's a way to show your love. And God is love, and even commands us to love, doesn't he? So how could sex be wrong?"

When you think about it, it's *technically true* that God is love and commands us to love, and that sex is about expressing love. But love cannot be achieved apart from what God has said is good—that is, apart from his commandments and his plan for our sexuality. That's where we see the almost undetectable twist I spoke of.

With this in mind, check out the first thing the serpent says to Eve: "Did God say, 'You shall not eat of *any* tree of the garden'?" Interestingly, the *King James Version* of the Bible uses the word "every" instead of "any." I believe this word better illustrates Satan's subtlety and intention here. Think about it: did God say that Adam and Eve couldn't eat of *every* tree in the garden? It turns out that indeed he did. God said that Adam and Eve could eat from *every tree but one*, and that means they can't eat from *every* tree. Enter the "spin zone."

FOCUSING ON THE NEGATIVE

The serpent knows full well that God had forbidden Adam and Eve from eating of the tree of the knowledge of good and evil. But the serpent *intends to make them think that they can achieve happiness apart from God's law of love, and that if they could only make their own rules and do whatever they wanted, then they would be truly happy.* Eve responds just the way we would expect (and the way we all probably would have responded): "We may eat of the fruit of the trees of the garden; but God said, 'You shall not eat of the fruit of the tree which is in the midst of the garden, neither shall you touch it, lest you die.'"

> **Did U Know**
>
> Many think Eve was alone at the tree, but Adam was right there with her. Scripture makes this clear by adding: "she also gave some to her husband, *who was with her* . . ." The reason for the addition of "who was with her" is that in the Bible's original language the serpent addresses the woman in the plural, as if he is speaking to *two* people.

At first glance, it might seem as though Adam and Eve merely perceive a mistake on the part of the serpent, and Eve, speaking for them both, is simply correcting him. But her response also reveals that Satan's subtlety has begun to work on their thinking. How so? He has gotten Adam and Eve to become so focused on the one thing they *are not* allowed to do that they lose sight of all the things they *are* allowed to do. True, God had told Adam and Eve not to eat from the fruit of the tree or they would die. But if you go back to Genesis 2:15–17, you'll find *he never said a single thing about touching it*! Adam and Eve had become fixated on the one thing they couldn't do, and it seemed so oppressive to them that they made it even bigger than it was.

You may have fallen into this trap before. I think we all have. Our parents say "no" to something we really want to do, and we, not thinking of the freedom they do give us, blow it out of proportion and say something like, "You never let me do *anything*. You hate me. You're so strict. You don't want me to have any fun. You want to ruin my life. I'm going, and there's nothing you can do to stop me." If we don't actually say these words, we think them. Well, that morning in the garden you could almost hear Adam and Eve's thoughts: "Our Father in heaven is so strict. He never lets us do anything. We can't even touch that tree. He's completely unreasonable. Let's take it anyway—he can't stop us!"

Remember, every other tree in the garden was theirs for the picking—just not this tree. This tree was off limits, and God had only kept them from it because he loved Adam and Eve, wanted them to have a happy life, and knew that eating of the tree brought *danger* and meant certain death. This is hardly the work of an oppressive parent. So, the serpent knows that to catch Adam and Eve, he also needs to make them forget how much God loves them and wants them to be happy. He needs to get Adam and Eve to think that their heavenly Father doesn't really know best, but that he, the serpent, is their friend and has the inside scoop. In other words, he needs to inflict them with a little "parental amnesia," *so they will forget that God has given them everything, and that besides him there is no other.*

FORGETTING THE FATHER'S LOVE

At some point in our lives we all suffer from "parental amnesia." We go from our parents being the ones who love us, keep us safe, and are the smartest and the strongest people in the world (you know, the whole "my dad can beat up your dad" thing) to our parents being the ones who don't know what they are talking about, are "out of touch," don't understand what we're going through, and want to keep us from making our own decisions. No longer feeling safe but smothered, we typically want our parents to just leave us alone (except when we need a ride or some money). Our friends then tend to take the place of our parents as the real authorities in life. This is usually when we begin to lose our "childhood innocence." We forget that our parents have seen a lot more of life than we or our friends have. We forget that probably no one in the world loves us, or want what's best for us, or want us to be happy more than they do, so we really can have confidence in their decisions (*confidence* comes from the Latin words *"con"* and *"fides,"* meaning "with faith or trust"). In my own case, my parents did wind up being right practically all the time, and I would have saved myself a lot of trouble if I hadn't "lost my memory."

Well, Satan wants Adam and Eve to lose their memory. He wants them to lose their innocence. He wants them to trust him as their friend and doubt God as their Father. The serpent's first approach: make it appear as though God doesn't know what he is talking about. "You will not die," the serpent said. Once again, *technically true*. Adam and Eve didn't eat the fruit and *physically* drop dead right then and there. Of course, they would eventually, but the serpent conveniently left that out. He also completely failed to mention the whole *spiritual death* thing that *would* happen then and there.

Satan's next move: get Adam and Eve to think that God really only cares about parental power, not love, that all he wants to do is spoil their fun and keep them from "growing up" and making their own choices. "God knows when you eat it you will be like him and can decide for yourself what's good and evil." In other words, "Grow up, be your own person, take a stand, take control of your life. What, are you going to let your Father make all your decisions for you?"

That's all Adam and Eve need to hear. They have the motivation, now all they need are the excuses. They see that the fruit is delicious, attractive, and could make them wise, and so they waste no time: they take some and eat it. At this point, Adam and Eve are primarily "thinking with their stomachs," that is, they are acting on their base instincts and drives. Hence, God's final lesson to Adam, *you are not an animal*, is undone as well. Animals by nature always act on instincts and drives, but human beings don't. As persons endowed with intellects and wills, human beings can "think before they act." According to the story, it seems as if Adam and Eve don't really want to give themselves time to think about their decision, lest they "flounder."

But they sure did flounder: hook, line, and sinker, right onto the deck of the serpent's fishing boat! *Sin, suffering, and death had entered into human history.* "The beginning" had come to an end. Forgetting the Father's love and turning their backs on him, Adam and Eve had lost their *original innocence*, and along with it, their chances for real love, true happiness, and a rich life.

JOHN PAUL II
In His Own Words

The man who picks the fruit of the tree of the knowledge of good and evil makes at the same time a fundamental choice and carries it through against the will of the Creator, God-Yahweh, by accepting the motivation suggested by the tempter. . . . This motivation clearly implies casting doubt on the Gift and on Love, from which creation takes its origin as gift.

(TOB 26:4)

THINGS TO PONDER AND SHARE

1. How does Genesis 3 reveal that Satan knows a thing or two about fishing? What are the lessons he wants Adam and Eve (and us) to "unlearn"?

2. Why can subtlety be much more dangerous than it seems? Give some examples of how people "spin" and distort the truth to get others to accept a particular point of view.

3. Has there ever been a time in your life when you have been tempted to pursue happiness apart from God's law? If so, when? What resulted?

4. Have you ever focused so much on what you are not allowed to do that you forgot about all the things you are allowed to do? Explain the situation.

5. Have you ever suffered from "parental amnesia"? Give one example.

6. Name a time when you didn't "think before you acted." Why did you do so? What was your decision based on?

·· READ THE CATECHISM OF THE CATHOLIC CHURCH ····

nos. 386–387, 391–401

CHAPTER 9

THE GREAT DIVORCE

The LORD God then called to the man and asked him: "Where are you?" He answered, "I heard you in the garden; but I was afraid, because I was naked, so I hid." . . . [To the man God said:] ". . . you are dust, and to dust you shall return."

—Genesis 3:9–10, 19 NAB

THE EFFECTS OF ORIGINAL SIN ON HUMANITY

The parable of the Prodigal Son in Luke's Gospel is one of my favorite passages in the Bible. It is also the theme of one of my favorite spiritual books, *The Return of the Prodigal Son* by Father Henri Nouwen. This parable is about a father who has two sons. The younger son does something that people of any time and culture would regard as an act of utter disrespect, even the equivalent of wishing his father dead: he asks for his share of the inheritance "in advance." The father's response would have astonished those who heard the parable, and it ought to astonish us. The father does not disown the son, he doesn't kick him out of the house, he doesn't punish him, and he doesn't even reprimand him or say, "How could you do this to me after all I have done for you?" The Scripture is stark: "So the father divided the property between them" (Lk 15:12 NAB). He gives his son the money and lets him leave. And if the father knew his boy at all, he probably knew what he was going to spend his money on (see Lk 15:13, 30). Yet, the father also knew he couldn't force his son to love him or make him stay. Loving the son meant letting him go. And that, I'm sure, wasn't easy. It probably broke the father's heart.

Of course, the father in the parable represents God. God knows that just as love requires the truth about what is good, it also requires the freedom to choose it. He didn't tell Adam and Eve not to eat the fruit of the tree and then tie their hands behind their backs or put duct tape over their mouths. If he did, their choice "not to eat" wouldn't have been a choice at all. No choice, no love. It's as simple as that. And because God wants us to love him, he takes that risk of creating us with freedom, a risk he knows might break his heart.

CHOICES ALWAYS HAVE CONSEQUENCES

Like Adam and Eve's "yes," our "yes" to God, which is also a "yes" to love, means nothing unless we can also say "no." Ultimately, however, our choice will have a consequence. *Choices always have consequences.* Some choices have *major consequences.* The prodigal son's choice did—he wound up hungry, homeless, and alone. Adam and Eve's choice certainly did.

God respects our choices so much that he lets us live (and die) with them and their consequences. The famous British writer C. S. Lewis (who wrote *The Lion, the Witch, and the Wardrobe*) said that ultimately this world has two types of people: the ones *who say to God*, "Thy will be done," and the ones *to whom God says*, "Thy will be done." [2]

Traditionally defined, sin is "an offense against God and his law." However, it can also be understood as "*a choice not to love* God with all of one's mind, heart, soul, and strength, and our neighbor as ourselves." By sin we turn away from "loving as God loves" and, therefore, turn away from the meaning of our existence and forfeit our personal happiness. If love means "communion," sin means "separation": separation from God, from others, and from our true selves.

The first earthly separation or "divorce," believe it or not, did not involve a man and a woman. It involved a man, a woman, and God. Adam and Eve divorced themselves from God. They ate from the fruit of the tree that God had forbidden. They chose licentiousness (a fancy term that means "doing whatever you want") and independence; to live for themselves and make their own rules. And God gave them the freedom to make that choice. He didn't force them to love him, and so he let his children walk away—even though he knew the trouble that was in store for them. It's the hardest thing a father has to do. (Sounds a bit like the father from the parable, doesn't it?)

When Adam and Eve divorced themselves from God and committed the *Original Sin*, they left all their hopes for being "like God" behind. In a sense, the irony of the serpent's enticement—"you will be like God"—is that Adam and Eve already *were* like God. The serpent made it seem as if they needed to grasp at divine life, but they had already received it as a gift. Adam and Eve should have responded to the serpent by saying, "Sorry. Been there, done that." But they didn't. By choosing to eat the forbidden fruit in order to be like God, they actually became *unlike* him.

FOR YOUR CONSIDERATION

Contrast this attitude of our first parents with that of Jesus, the New Adam, who "though he was in the form of God, did not count equality with God a thing to be grasped" (Phil 2:6).

HUMAN NATURE: OUT OF ORDER

When God created Adam and Eve, he endowed them with souls (having the powers of intellect and will) *and* bodies. Their intellects were supposed to know the good and direct their wills to choose it. Their souls would then direct their bodies toward right action. This "order" or *hierarchy* within a human person would exist as long as his or her soul remained in communion with God.

When they ate from the fruit of the tree, however, and rejected God as their true Other and the Lord of life, their entire world began to unravel like a thread pulled from a sweater. Divorced from God, their very nature as body-persons became so *disordered* that loving as God loves in and through their bodies became virtually impossible. The order that existed *within* their souls, as well as the order that existed *between* their bodies and their souls, was thrown into disarray. Satan, the first rebel, had instigated Adam and Eve's rebellion against God. Adam and Eve's rebellion in turn caused an uprising or rebellion within their own persons. Their intellects no longer submitted to what was good. Their wills no longer obeyed their intellects. And their bodies no longer followed the directions of their souls. You could say that sin turned everything "inside out and upside down," and caused human nature to be "out of order."

Adam's response to God after eating the fruit reveals this disorder: "I was afraid, because I was naked, so I hid myself." Adam's own words show that the relationship of his soul to his body had been damaged. In fact, because of Original Sin, human beings had now become "damaged goods." They were still fundamentally good since they were made by God, and a spark of God's original plan still flickered in them, but they had become "psychosomatically challenged." They wanted to know good and evil, but their intellects had become so confused that they lost much of their ability to know good and evil when they saw it. They wanted to make their own decisions, but their wills had become so weak that, even if their intellects knew what was good, they had lost much of their ability to choose it (see Rom 7:19, 22–23). They wanted to be free and "like God," but their souls had become such slaves to the instincts and drives of their bodies that they had become more like the animals. They wanted to "gain the whole world" and "lost their own souls," as well as Paradise, in the process.

Yet, this is the life they chose. *Human choices are self-determining*, which simply means that our choices make us who we are. There are two kinds of human dignity: the kind *God gives us* and we *already have* simply by virtue of being made in his image, and the kind we *give ourselves* and *achieve* by our free choices.[3] You may have heard the saying: "Sow an act, reap a habit. Sow a habit, reap a character. Sow a character, reap a destiny."[4] C. S. Lewis once said that by our choices we make ourselves into either a heavenly or hellish creature, and that when we die we simply go where we belong.[5] Humans are the only beings who can choose NOT to be what they were created to be. A tree can't choose not to be a tree; a dog

> Saint Paul discusses the experience of our "out of order" nature when he states:
>
> "I do not understand my own actions. For I do not do what I want, but I do the very thing I hate. . . . So I find it to be a law that when I want to do right, evil lies close at hand. For I delight in the law of God, in my inmost self, but I see in my members another law at war with the law of my mind and making me captive to the law of sin which dwells in my members" (Rom 7:15, 21–24).

can't choose not to be a dog; but a human can choose not to be human. A human being can choose not to be the "image and likeness of God" he or she was created to be from "the beginning." And the road to inhumanity starts with a single choice.

DEATH: THE ULTIMATE CONSEQUENCE OF SIN

Now, besides being "out of order," another thing happened when Adam and Eve divorced themselves from God: they were "doomed to die," because God was their source of life. Their souls had separated from God, so one day they would also separate from their bodies— the ultimate insult to body-persons. Their bodies would "return to the dirt," and their souls would be consigned to a dismal eternal existence since they would be separated from God, who is their supreme good and ultimate happiness (or, as theologians would say, beatitude). Death is the natural consequence of sin. Believe it or not, it is also its appropriate punishment. As Saint Paul said, "The wages of sin is death" (Rom 6:23).

Did you know that the seriousness of a crime is determined not only by "what is done" but by "to whom it is done"? Well, what if the person offended is God? That would make the crime *infinitely serious*. Since God is an infinite and eternal Person, the punishment would have to be infinite and eternal in order for it to fit the crime. That's where death comes in. The *bad news* is that, since humans are finite beings, there's nothing they can ever do to "redeem themselves." Finite beings can never make up for an infinite offense. Not even the death of every human being who ever lived or will ever live, added together, could do that. No, humans would need a Redeemer, a Savior. They would need someone who was human and could pay the debt on their behalf, but who also was infinite and could "afford" the debt they needed to pay. They would also need someone who could put the pieces of their human nature back together again. They would need the God-man. And God so desires for human beings to be reconciled to him, he so desires for human beings to fulfill the meaning and purpose of their existence and be happy, that he meets that need head-on! That's the *Good News*!

But let's not get too far ahead of ourselves. We're not done with Genesis quite yet.

JOHN PAUL II
In His Own Words

[T]he words, "I was afraid, because I am naked," . . . highlight the consequences of the fruit of the tree of the knowledge of good and evil in man's innermost [being]. These words reveal a certain constitutive fracture in the human person's interior. . . . The body is not subject to the spirit as in the state of original innocence, but carries within itself a constant hotbed of resistance against the spirit.

(TOB 28:2, 28:3)

THINGS TO PONDER AND SHARE

1. Have you ever misused your freedom and made a big mistake? What was it? What were the consequences?

2. Explain why our "yes" or "no" to our heavenly Father is simultaneously a "yes" or "no" to love.

3. How does sin "divorce" us from God, others, and our true selves?

4. Name a time when you knew the right thing to do but had a really hard time doing it.

5. Sometimes our bodies "tell" us to do something we know isn't good for us. When has this happened to you? How did you deal with it?

6. Give examples from history, society, or your personal experience of how our choices make us "who we are."

·· READ THE CATECHISM OF THE CATHOLIC CHURCH ·····

nos. 402–405, 1707

CHAPTER 10

FASHION STATEMENTS

Then the eyes of both of them were opened, and they knew that they were naked; so they sewed fig leaves together and made loincloths for themselves. When they heard the sound of the LORD God walking about in the garden at the breezy time of the day, the man and his wife hid themselves from the LORD God among the trees of the garden.

—Genesis 3:7–8 NAB

THE ENTRANCE OF LUST AND SHAME

"Beauty is in the eye of the beholder." "Don't judge a book by its cover." "Beauty isn't only skin deep." These are all variations on the same lesson we've heard a thousand times before. It's inspired countless works in literature, theater, and film, including the classic fable "Beauty and the Beast" by Madame Leprince de Beaumont, the literary masterpiece *Jane Eyre* by Charlotte Bronte, and

Shrek, the irreverent animated film. Have you ever wondered, though, why we constantly need to be reminded of this truth?

Well, after eating the fruit of the tree of the knowledge of good and evil, Adam and Eve began to have serious vision problems. I have always found it interesting that the biblical author chose the phrase: "Then the eyes of both of them were opened." Their eyes may have been opened, but they definitely weren't seeing 20/20. In fact, they had become radically nearsighted. They couldn't see past themselves. Their sin had caused lust to fill their hearts, which in turn distorted their perception of the world and each other.

The man and woman who were *created for love* had become the man and woman who were *conquered by lust*. As such, Adam and Eve could no longer easily see each other as *body-persons* made in the image of God, who have the right "to be treated as an object of love, and not as an object of use."[6] Instead, they were inclined to view each other as *simply bodies*; as objects to be used for their own purposes. They no longer readily beheld the beauty of each other's person; in fact, they *depersonalized* one another. Love says, "I *give myself* for *your* own sake." Lust says, "I *take you* for *my* own sake."

Now, it is important that, when we see the word "lust," we do not automatically equate its meaning with sexual immorality. The technical term is *concupiscence*, which refers to desires that are "out of order" because they incline us to thoughts, words, or deeds that are opposed to God's plan. This is why when Saint John Paul II discusses lust he refers to the "threefold lust" mentioned in the First Letter of John: *the lust of the flesh, the lust of the eyes*, and *the pride of life* (see 1 Jn 2:16–17 NJB). I find the way these are translated in the *New Jerusalem Bible* to be helpful: "*disordered bodily desires, disordered desires of the eyes*, and *pride in possession*." It's the "disordered desires of the eyes" that move us to see others as things or objects; to view one another as "just bodies" and not body-persons. "Pride in possession" motivates us to dominate others and possess them for our own selfish purposes. It also causes us to place too much value on material things. Finally, "disordered bodily desires" direct our actions toward the pursuit of physical pleasure and make pleasure-seeking our primary goal in life.

Realizing they were infected by this threefold lust, Adam and Eve "sewed fig leaves together and made loincloths for themselves" (Gen 3:7). Before sin they were "naked without shame." After sin they were "naked and ashamed." But why?

ASHAMED OF THEIR LUST

Contrary to popular belief, Adam and Eve weren't ashamed of their bodies—they were ashamed of the lust that had crept into their hearts. They were ashamed because they knew it shouldn't be there, yet they couldn't get rid of it. Sin had "disabled" their nature. Adam no longer saw Eve's person; for him, her beauty was "only skin deep." She became just a body, an "object" he could use and dominate: "your husband . . . shall rule over you." He would exploit and manipulate her for his own pleasure, as in the classic line, "If you loved me, you would . . ." But he knew in the depths of his being that exploiting her was wrong. And he was ashamed.

Eve for her part used Adam. Eve learned pretty quickly how to get Adam to do what she wanted. She would *get* control by making him *lose* control. She would have her own needs met, and she would do whatever it took—*even allow herself to be used*. But she knew in the depths of her being that using him was wrong. And she was ashamed.

If you don't get what I am saying, imagine your typical school dance. What do you see? How do the guys look at the girls? How are the girls dressed and why? What does the atmosphere encourage? What does the dancing resemble? And what's it all for? Don't you think guys and girls leave those dances "ashamed," with their integrity knocked down a few pegs? I know I've seen my share of tears, quarrels, confusion, fear, and disillusionment.

The truth is that after the first sin even sex itself became dissatisfying. Though sex is still good (God created it, after all), lust keeps it from being everything God intended it to be from "the beginning." Sure, the drives are still there. The physical sensation is still there. But the end result isn't joy. That's because the union of persons no longer seems accomplished in the union of bodies—and our hearts really long for the union of persons. Selfish motives—some conscious, some not—block total self-giving. The more this is the case, the shallower the "pleasure" and the more intense the shame. The biblical narrative indicates that, generally speaking, women are more "in touch" with and affected by this lack of communion, and yearn for something more: "your desire shall be for your husband." This in no way means that guys aren't and don't; it's just less apparent in guys and they tend not to notice the lack of communion as much. Guys tend to *replace* bodily union for personal union. Yet most guys still truly seek personal union, whether they realize it or not. *Girls confuse love for sex; guys confuse sex for love.* All too often, however, this confusion becomes a source of selfish manipulation: *Guys use love for sex; girls use sex for love.* And neither gets what they are looking for.

FOR YOUR CONSIDERATION

This is the first time Adam is referred to as Eve's husband. Here we see a contrast between the man who *cleaves* to his wife and the husband who *dominates* her. According to Saint John Paul II, the biblical author expressly used the term "husband" to accentuate the violation of God's original plan, not to justify man's domination of woman (see TOB 30).

Do you remember when I said that men and women were created to *complement* each other? It should be obvious that after sin that *original complementarity* became a *historical conflict.* "The beginning" ended, and the "battle of the sexes" began. History is replete with examples of women's oppression, and there are still inequalities today. Distorted ideas about masculinity and femininity persist. Presently, alongside a genuine feminism that celebrates womanhood and works for social justice, a distorted view has gained prominence that denies the difference and complementarity between men and women, sees gender as merely a social construct, and identifies abortion rights with women's rights (even though statistically half of all babies aborted are girls).

What else could Adam and Eve do but cover up? It was the only way to protect themselves *from themselves* and from each other. But, in a way, being "clothed with shame" and being "clothed with fig leaves" also reveal that Adam and Eve were still "fashionable." They still had something to work with. Adam and Eve had not lost God's original plan entirely. A hint of it was left, an echo if you will. They could still detect it; they could still hear it, even though lust had clouded their vision and clogged their ears. Neither the serpent nor their sin had been able to drive God's original plan from them fully. And they dressed accordingly.

In this way, shame has a positive effect: it attempts to preserve the spousal meaning of the body. It helps us to see our bodies as the way in which we give ourselves to others and express love. It causes human beings to regard the body with the dignity it deserves, since the body reveals the person. In short, when we protect our bodies, we protect ourselves.

For this reason, the *virtue of modesty*—which "inspires one's choice of clothing" to guide "how one looks at others and behaves toward them"—doesn't have anything to do with the body being "dirty." It has everything to do with body-persons being beautiful images of God. Modesty protects the person. Modesty helps us to "perceive the person." By "wearing loincloths," we divert attention from our private parts and once again learn to "look into each other's eyes" and see into each other's souls. In the process, we not only protect ourselves from the lustful gaze of others, but we help others not to gaze lustfully. It's not love but lust that says, "If you've got it, flaunt it." Flaunting can also be a cry for attention, a misguided attempt to be noticed and affirmed, or even a way to try to assert your sexual value over others of your own gender. The sad part is that this is often self-defeating, and only worsens our sense of self-worth and intensifies our feelings of loneliness. And this goes for both guys and girls.

THE FEAR OF BEING EXPOSED

Now, fear almost always accompanies shame. The first thing Adam and Eve do after they "cover up" is "run for cover"—they bolt for the forest when they hear God approaching. When we are ashamed, we rarely want anybody else to discover what we're ashamed of. Adam and Eve didn't want each other to find out about the lust that had crept into their hearts. But that doesn't work with God. The Scriptures say that God knows everything in our minds and hearts (see Ps 44:20–21, 139; Jn 2:25).

The Scriptures also say that "everyone who does evil hates the light, and does not come to the light, lest his deeds should be exposed" (Jn 3:20). Well, "God is light" (1 Jn 1:5). Even if we don't come to the light, eventually it will come to us. That's what happened with Adam and Eve. They knew that they had done evil and had disobeyed the God who created the universe. But instead of remembering that he was also the God who loved them completely and that "there is no fear in love" (1 Jn 4:18), they forgot this, lost trust in his love, and ran away. I don't think they ever imagined that he would search for them. But that is what love does. "Where are you?" God asks (as if he didn't know).

Rather than take responsibility and ask for forgiveness, however, Adam and Eve try to avoid it. Shame almost always goes hand in hand with denial. Let's face it, we are very quick to take responsibility for the good things we do: good grades, sports accomplishments, success in the arts, good deeds to the poor, etc. We love to say, "Look what I did!" We never say something like, "I really can't take credit for that. I mean, my intelligence is genetic, my parents have instilled good discipline habits in me, and my teachers are masterful and have taught me great studying techniques." Conversely, however, *we are rarely willing to take responsibility for the bad things we do.* We usually find somebody to blame: "So and so told me to do it," or "I didn't know" (i.e., "No one told me"), or "Everybody else was doing it," or "The test was unfair—the teacher didn't cover the material," etc. It's funny; we say we want *absolute freedom and independence* with regard to our choices, when what we really want is absolute freedom from *the consequences* of our choices. But we can't have it both ways. If we're responsible for the good we do, then we're responsible for the bad as well.

THE BLAME GAME

So, Adam and Eve go from *shame* to *blame*. God confronts Adam with his sin, and Adam blames Eve and, implicitly, he also blames God: "That *woman* that *you* created made me do it. Some helper she turned out to be." God then confronts Eve, and she blames the serpent and, implicitly, God and Adam: "The serpent tricked me. By the way, didn't *you* create him? And Adam, you were right there with me—why didn't you say something? Why didn't you do something to stop me?"

The blame game is a very big part of the battle of the sexes. It becomes very obvious when a couple gets divorced. The children are often caught in between and get the "low down" from each parent about everything that's wrong with the other. It's incredibly painful to watch, and even more painful to live. It's such a real-life drama that it has inspired many major motion pictures.

But the blame game is being played wherever the battle of the sexes rages. To avoid responsibility for our actions with regard to sex, I have heard such excuses as, "When she dresses like that, how can I resist?" "But he told me he loves me." "Why did God give me these hormones, anyway?"

We've certainly come quite a distance from seeing each other as the "helpers" God fashioned us to be. And though we're ashamed of ourselves, there's still hope. Not all has been lost. God's original plan still echoes in our hearts.

JOHN PAUL II
In His Own Words

[Lustful] "desiring" . . . indicates an experience of the value of the body in which its spousal meaning ceases to be spousal. . . . What also ceases is its procreative meaning.

(TOB 39:5)

One can even say that, through shame, man and woman almost remain in the state of original innocence. In fact, they continually become conscious of the spousal meaning of the body and intend to protect it, so to speak, from concupiscence [lust].

(TOB 31:1)

THINGS TO PONDER AND SHARE

1. What are some ways that beauty is not just "skin deep"? Does our society value them? Why or why not?

2. How should we understand "lust" and what is a common misperception of it? What is the threefold lust? Explain each of the three "lusts" and how they are related.

3. Make a list of examples from history, past or present, and from everyday situations that demonstrate the "battle of the sexes."

4. Do you think guys and girls manipulate one another to get what they want? If so, in what ways? Have you ever witnessed this in your own life or in the lives of those around you? If so, when?

5. What are some ways in which guys and girls can help one another "perceive the person" through practicing the virtue of modesty?

6. Have you ever played the blame game? When and why?

· · READ THE CATECHISM OF THE CATHOLIC CHURCH · · · · ·

nos. 369–370, 2521–2524

CHAPTER 11

HEARTS TOO HARD TO LOVE

They said to [Jesus], "Why then did Moses command one to give a certificate of divorce, and to put her away?" He said to them, "For your hardness of heart Moses allowed you to divorce your wives, but from the beginning it was not so."

—Matthew 19:7–8

Aristotle, the ancient Greek philosopher we have already discussed, held that "art imitates life." Fyodor Dostoyevsky, the famous Russian novelist and author of *Crime and Punishment* and *The Brothers Karamazov*, is credited with saying, "At first, art imitates life. Then life will imitate art." Whatever the case may be, when we consider the messages that are being sent about life, love, marriage, and sex in many of the books, magazines, songs, movies, and TV shows that are "mainstream" today, it seems clear that *sin is "in," and God's original plan is "out."*

Now that we have looked at Satan's fishing technique, sin, and sin's devastating impact on human nature, we can easily understand why distorted messages are so prevalent and why we appear to be so far from God's original plan for life, love, marriage, and sex. Satan's subtlety is still at work in the world. If he can get you to hum the tune, laugh out loud, or make you root for the main characters to "hook up," then he's "hooked" *you.* Sometimes all Satan needs to do is desensitize us and get us to believe that sexual sin is "no big deal" and not all that harmful.

When we look around us, it may seem as though our world overvalues sex. No matter where you turn, it's "in your face," right? You just have to walk through your local shopping mall to be bombarded with the clothing or underwear displays. Or just walk through the grocery store checkout line and catch the gossip and fashion magazines: who's having an affair with whom in Hollywood or Washington and, of course, there's those sexualized (less than half-dressed) women and men and articles like "10 Tricks to Drive Your Man Crazy" and "All the New Great Sex Tips You'll Want to Know."

Actually, our world places *too little* value on sex. Think about it. Today sex often becomes primarily about seeking physical pleasure. For all intents and purposes, it's a recreational activity, like any other. There are videos to help you with your golf swing, and there are videos to help you "spice up your sex life." People often judge each other mostly in terms of their sexual desirability. And it has also become generally socially acceptable to commit practically any sort of sexual act with just about anyone, as long as everybody agrees. Things don't seem much different among teens. It appears that "hooking up" (a vague term that means everything from "making out" to oral sex) has become more common among teens than "going out" (dating). Some social media seem to encourage and enable the "hook up" culture. And then there's "pornography in your pocket," with Internet porn as close as your phone's touchscreen, and viewing it being socially accepted. Not much is taboo anymore.

So our world isn't oversexed—it's *undersexed*! Just like Adam and Eve, people today miss the point of sex entirely. They miss what being created *male and female* is all about. They miss what being *body-persons* is all about. They miss what the *life-giving communion of persons* that God created a husband and wife to express through their sexual union is all about.

HARD HEARTS, REBELLIOUS HEARTS

To return to Jesus' conversation with the Pharisees, his response to their question wasn't directed only to them. When Jesus said, "for your hardness of heart," he meant your heart and my heart as well. Basically, Jesus was saying that apart from God, *the human heart has become too hard to love*.

In the Scriptures, the phrase "hardness of heart" refers generally to a person's rebellion against God. It also refers to the resulting *state of separation*—our being "out of order." Therefore, "hardness of heart" can be taken to refer to Original Sin and its negative impact on our nature.

With this in mind, the meaning of Jesus' words becomes clear. When Jesus said to the Pharisees, "for your hardness of heart," he meant, "because of sin." It's as if he were saying, "You were made in my image to love as I love and to give the sincere gift of yourselves in and through your bodies. But sin devastated your ability to do that. So, recognizing your limitations, Moses made an exception for you. But that wasn't part of my original plan for life, love, marriage, and sex."

I mentioned in the last chapter that God's original plan still echoes in the depths of our being. We still aspire to true and lasting happiness. We still desire to love and be loved. We still basically want goodness and justice. We still search for God. But now we are inclined to look for happiness in temporary pleasures. Lust and uncontrolled emotions often masquerade as real love. Selfish motives and moral relativism corrupt goodness and justice. And we tend to make God and religion into whatever suits our fancy or brings us comfort at the time.

HAPPINESS LOST

All of this, of course, has a direct effect on both our earthly and eternal happiness, since it contradicts everything we were made for from "the beginning." When you think about it, after Original Sin human beings are really in quite a pathetic situation.

We started by saying:

1. To be happy, we need to be fully human.
2. To be fully human, we need to be the image and likeness of God that we were created to be.
3. To be the image and likeness of God that we were created to be, we need to love as God loves and give the sincere gift of ourselves in and through our bodies.
4. Therefore, to be happy we need to love as God loves and give the sincere gift of ourselves in and through our bodies.

But then we learned about the entrance of Original Sin and its effect on human nature.

1. Sin makes it practically impossible for us to love as God loves and give the sincere gift of ourselves in and through our bodies.
2. Therefore, sin makes it practically impossible for us to be the image and likeness of God that we were created to be.
3. Therefore, sin makes it practically impossible for us to be fully human.
4. Therefore, sin makes it practically impossible for us to be happy.

In reaching for happiness apart from God and his law of love, Adam and Eve lost their happiness, true love, and God. This is the paradox of sin: it promises fulfillment, but brings emptiness; it promises freedom, but brings slavery; it promises "heaven," but brings hell.

Even worse, Original Sin is not just an event—it's a condition. When Adam and Eve had children, they passed their damaged (sometimes called *fallen*) nature on to them, as well as the unhappiness that came with it. And there's none of that "skipping a genera-tion" thing. Since we are all descendants of Adam and Eve, *all human beings* have the condition or dis-order known as Original Sin. All, that is, except for the New Adam and New Eve, who begin the new humanity that will live by the new law of love (which really isn't so much a *new* law as the *original* law God had made from "the beginning").

Although God allowed human beings to suffer the consequences of sin in their lives, he never stopped car-ing for them. One of the first things God did after punish-ing Adam and Eve was make them better clothes—nice, new, leather ones (see Gen 3:21). And even in the midst of his punishments, God made a promise to human-ity. He promised that he would send a Savior to "strike at the head" of the serpent and redeem human beings from the power of sin and death (see Gen 3:15).

If sin and its devastating effects were the end of the story, we wouldn't call God's plan for us "Good News," would we? Humanity's got to make its comeback.

And indeed it does.

JOHN PAUL II
In His Own Words

[As a result of Original Sin] the structure of communion among the persons disappears; both human beings become almost incapable of reaching the interior measure of the heart directed toward the freedom of the gift and the spousal meaning of the body, which is intrinsic [essential] to that measure.

(TOB 33:1)

THINGS TO PONDER AND SHARE

1. What are some of the *subtle* and *not so subtle* messages out there today about life, love, marriage, and sex? Give specific media-related examples from advertisements, commercials, TV shows, movies, and music.

2. What are some ways in which sex seems to be everywhere you turn?

3. How does our society actually place *too little* rather than *too much* value on sex?

4. How has the human heart become too hard to love? What are some examples of this?

5. Outline the connection between our personal happiness and the need to love as God loves and give the sincere gift of ourselves in and through our bodies. How does sin corrupt this?

6. Even with the apparently hopeless situation that sin has caused, why can we still have hope for the future?

··READ THE CATECHISM OF THE CATHOLIC CHURCH····

nos. 388, 407–412, 1608–1610, 2515

CHAPTER 12

THE DIVINE DO-OVER

Then as one man's trespass led to condemnation for all men, so one man's act of righteousness leads to acquittal and life for all men. For as by one man's disobedience many were made sinners, so by one man's obedience many will be made righteous.

—Romans 5:18–19

JESUS CHRIST BRINGS US BACK TO THE BEGINNING

As young boys attending elementary school, we looked forward to nothing more in our day than lunch recess. We would practically inhale our food so we could be the first out the door. At my school, lunch recess meant kickball. And let me tell you, it was pretty intense. We even kept stats. Inevitably, however, at least once every recess we would get into some dispute over a call. It typically went something like this:

"He was safe."

"No, he was out."

"Tie goes to the runner."

"But I got him just before he put his foot on the base."

This would continue for a couple of minutes until everyone's tempers were sufficiently flaring. A scuffle often occurred—like I said, it was *intense*! The recess monitors would gradually move to the scene, and then someone, most likely frustrated by the loss of precious recess time, would shout out: "DO-OVER!"

With these words, the debate would stop cold. Everyone would nonchalantly go back to where they started, and we would do the play all over again. It worked every single time. And generally all was forgotten (unless you were on the losing team and had to hear the "We're number one" cheer all the way back to class).

I have already mentioned that human beings need a Savior. We need someone who can pay the infinite debt that we incurred for sin but can't "afford" to pay. We need someone who can put the pieces of our broken nature back together again. We need someone who can heal our brokenness and make us whole again, as well as heal our relationships with God and others (interestingly, the Latin root for salvation is *salus*, which means health or wholeness). We need someone who can restore God's original plan for human beings and bring us back to "the beginning" so we can be fully human and find true happiness.

We need the New Adam (Jesus) and the New Eve (Mary/the Church) to begin the new humanity (the baptized) that will live by the new law of love (the Great Commandment/the Beatitudes), which is really the original law from "the beginning."

In order for humanity to go back to "the beginning," the New Adam and the New Eve must go back first. Jesus and Mary must *redo* everything that the first Adam and Eve did, but do it the right way, so they can *undo* everything that the first Adam and Eve did wrong. The technical name for this is the redemption, but you could call it the divine do-over.

The bird's-eye view of the divine do-over goes something like this: Adam's "no" to God, which "led to condemnation for all people," was made possible through Eve's "no" to God. Likewise, Jesus' "yes" to God, which "leads to acquittal and life for all people," is made possible by Mary's "yes" to God (often called her *fiat*). But if we take a moment to "zoom in," we'll find some pretty amazing things.

Adam and Eve chose their will (what they decided was good and evil) over the Father's will in the Garden

> **Did U Know**
>
> Jesus taught that Baptism is necessary for salvation (Jn 3:5; *CCC*, no. 1257). However, in addition to the "baptism of water," the Church has understood that there is also the "baptism of blood," the "baptism of explicit desire," and the "baptism of implicit desire" (see *CCC*, nos. 1258–1260).
>
> These baptisms can "substitute" for the baptism of water where it is not possible for some reason.

of Eden, refusing to love as God loves and give the sincere gift of themselves in and through their bodies. Due to this, Adam and Eve were destined to die and suffer the separation of their bodies and souls for all eternity. In addition, Adam and Eve transmitted death and a damaged nature to all human beings, since all human beings are "relatives" of Adam and Eve. This human nature is so damaged that it makes us practically incapable of loving as God loves and giving the sincere gift of ourselves in and through our bodies.

Jesus and Mary, on the other hand, chose the Father's will (what God decided is good and evil) over their will in the Garden of Gethsemane (Jesus) and the garden in Nazareth (Mary). They both loved as God loves in and through their bodies by giving the sincere gift of themselves: Jesus by offering his body on the Cross and Mary by offering her body (and womb) as the mother of Jesus. Due to this, they were destined to live and enjoy the reunification of their bodies and souls for all eternity: Jesus in his resurrection and Mary in her assumption. And by becoming "relatives" of Jesus and Mary in Baptism, new life and a redeemed nature is transmitted to us. This redeemed nature makes us capable, because of God's grace, of loving as God loves and giving the sincere gift of ourselves in and through our bodies.

When we discover these "details" of the divine do-over, we can see clearly how our redemption—which includes the redemption of our bodies—is accomplished. First, you may notice that Mary, the New Adam's mother, is compared with Eve, the first Adam's wife. It's not important that Jesus and Mary were not husband and wife, as Adam and Eve were. What's important is that they are the "new man" and the "new woman." Jesus and Mary are the "model" man and woman, and everything that man and woman were supposed to be from "the beginning." *That's why they can give humanity a "new beginning."*

In addition, Mary, as the one who "housed" Christ in the "tabernacle" of her womb and bore him for the world, was a "model" of the Church. In fact, many of the same titles we give to Mary are also given to the Church, and vice versa. Maybe you've heard someone say "Holy Mother Church." Therefore, the Church can also be understood as the "New Eve." *The Church is the Bride of the New Adam* (Jn 3:27–29; Eph 5:21–33), and, as such, she becomes *the Mother of the faithful* who are reborn as sons and daughters of God from her "womb" in the waters of Baptism (Gal 4:4–7; Titus 3:4–7).

And that's where we come in.

> **Did U Know**
>
> Mary is sometimes referred to as "co-redemptrix" or "cooperator in the redemption," and one of the church's titles is the "Sacrament of Salvation." This doesn't mean that Mary redeemed us or that the Church saves us—obviously, Jesus does this. However, Jesus redeems us through Mary's "fiat" and saves us through the Church.

THE SACRAMENT OF BAPTISM

The day of our Baptism was the day "the greatest story ever told" became *our* story. It was the day when the divine do-over became *our* do-over.

I know that most of us were baptized as babies and probably don't remember it, but that was the most significant day in our lives. It was even more significant than the day we were born (although, obviously, that was a prerequisite). On the day of our baptism, *everything changed* for us. We received a *new identity* and *new family*, and with it a *new power* and a *new hope* for the future. We also received a *new standard*: God's original plan from "the beginning." In Baptism, Jesus literally brought us "back to the beginning" and gave us a "new beginning."

So, how did Baptism accomplish all of this? At the very moment the water was poured over our heads, the Holy Spirit came into our hearts and we became identified with Jesus Christ and all he accomplished in the divine do-over. We were joined to his saving death and resurrection in such a real and profound way that *we actually died and rose with him* (see Rom 6:4–11). It's almost as if we were transported back in time and, in an instant, lived through the death and resurrection along with Jesus. This enabled *us* to receive *his merits* and reap the benefits of *his accomplishments* in the divine do-over. Pretty "mind-blowing," huh? That's because it's a *mystery*, and, as such, is always beyond our total understanding. But one thing is for sure: it is very, very good news!

BECOMING ANOTHER CHRIST

For all intents and purposes, this means that we have become *identified* with Jesus Christ; that *his* identity has become *our* identity. Therefore, each of us who has been baptized is, in a sense, *another Christ*. The Original Sin that marred our ability to live as God's image in the world and kept us from earthly and eternal happiness was forgiven, and we became the new man or the new woman, the visible "image of the invisible God" (Col 1:15) who has "hope of eternal life" (Titus 3:7). We became the son or daughter of God by being "born of water and the Spirit" (Jn 3:5). As a result, we became members of the *People of God* and the *Family of God*, that is, the Church.

In a nutshell, through our "new beginning" in Baptism, we became everything we were created to be from "the beginning" *and more*! As a result, we are called and commanded to live as Jesus lived, (see 1 Jn 2:6), love as Jesus loves (see Jn 15:12), and be holy as he is holy (see 1 Pet 1:14–16). Jesus himself set the *new standard*, and he is the yardstick by which we are to measure ourselves.

You may be thinking, "Then I'll never 'measure up.' That's an impossible standard." On one level you're absolutely right. We live as if in a tension between the first Adam and the last Adam. We are still left to battle the negative effects of sin on our nature and the influence of a world where "sin is in." The devil still "prowls around like a roaring lion" waiting to devour us (1 Pet 5:8). Each day we must fight temptation. Each day we must struggle against the tendency to lust instead of love and be selfish instead of selfless. Each day we must work to "put away the old self" (Eph 4:22 NAB) and "not be conformed to this world" (Rom 12:2). We become the new man or new woman in Baptism, but we also must become the new man or the new woman by the choices we make every day. That requires major effort on our part. Working out our salvation is a difficult task (see Phil 2:12). It demands a life-long process and a long, hard road. Let's face it, if left to our own power and abilities (or rather, our own powerlessness and inabilities due to Original Sin), we would fail miserably. And we *do* fail miserably. But there's more good news.

NOTABLE QUOTABLE

You see how many are the benefits of Baptism . . . we have enumerated ten honors [it bestows]. For this reason we baptize even infants, though they are not defiled by [personal] sins, so that there may be given to them holiness, righteousness, adoption, inheritance, brotherhood with Christ, and that they may be his [Christ's] members.

—Saint John Chrysostom

First, as Pope Francis has reminded us, "the name of God is Mercy." We are *loved sinners*. We are imperfect and limited human beings, and it is important to know that God doesn't love us because we are perfect but because we are his beloved children. So when you fail and are tempted to get discouraged, do not forget the Father's love and run away as Adam and Eve did. Trust in God's love for you—a love that accepts you for all you are and all you're aren't. Second, along with the *new identity* and *new standard* we have received, we have received a *new power*: Jesus' power! We can do all things through Christ who strengthens us (see Phil 4:13). For human beings it is impossible to be the new man or the new woman and live accordingly. But "with God all things are possible" (Mt 19:26; Mk 10:27; Lk 1:37). We are not in it alone.

HELP FROM HEAVEN

In order to understand this better, let's use an analogy that Jesus used: a yoke. A yoke is a harness-like contraption that is fixed around the necks of oxen and attached to a plow for the oxen to pull. A yoke typically accommodates two oxen, so if one ox tires and can't pull the plow, the other ox will pick up the slack and finish the job. When Jesus says, "Take my yoke upon you . . . for my yoke is easy and my burden is light" (Mt 11:29–30), he is saying that being redeemed by him is like being "yoked" to him. He is in one side and we are in the other. And when, due to the effects of Original Sin, we find it difficult (or maybe even practically impossible) to love as God loves, Jesus "picks up the slack," provides what we lack, and *gives us grace* so that sin will not have dominion over us and we can "finish the job."

How does Jesus do this? He gives us a "helper" to *reorder* our inside-out and upside-down nature, to *recreate* us in his image, and to make up for what we lack (see Jn 14:16–17, 26). He gives us a "helper" who will ultimately *empower us to be the "helpers" God intended us to be for one another from "the beginning" as husband and wife*! This "helper" is the Holy Spirit, and we received him into our hearts on the day we were baptized! That's right: the same Holy Spirit who moved over the waters and created the world, the same Holy Spirit who was breathed into Adam and made him a living being, the same Holy Spirit who raised Jesus from the dead—dwells in us! Now that's real "power for living." Actually, it's real *power for loving*.

Remember how we said that the Holy Spirit is the "love of the Father and the Son" in the heart of the Trinity? That means that when we receive the Holy Spirit in Baptism, the "love of God" or *God's own love* comes to dwell in our hearts (see Rom 5:5). This divine love *gives us the power to "love as God loves"*: to give the sincere gift of ourselves in and through our bodies. He *enlightens our intellects* so we can once again know the truth about what is good. He *strengthens our wills* so we can choose it. He *quells the disordered bodily desires that pull us away from God's plan* so that the body will obey the commands of the soul. He transforms our bodies into "temples" through which we can offer ourselves in love as a "living sacrifice," just as Jesus did: "This is my body given for you." Yes, *we really can "love as Jesus (God) loves,"* because the "love with which the Father loves the Son and the Son loves the Father" is our "helper"! And if we can love as God loves, then we can fulfill the purpose of our existence as human beings and finally find the happiness we've been searching for. And what can be better than that?

However, it should be fairly obvious that this doesn't happen all at once. Baptism isn't like a magic wand that is waved over you and—"presto change-o"—you are perfect. On your baptismal day, you probably couldn't even talk or walk. Just as we grow and mature in our "natural" or physical life, we have to grow and mature in our *"supernatural"* or *spiritual life*, that is, in the *new life* we have been given in Christ. The two main ways we do this are through *prayer* and *receiving the sacraments*.

PRAYER

Prayer can be defined as "the raising of one's mind and heart to God or the requesting of good things from God."[7] It can also be understood as communication with God who is our friend.[8] As such, communion with God is its goal. In relationships, the goal of communication is always communion. The more you communicate with someone, the closer the two of you become. Just think of your closest friend and the hours you spend either on the phone or texting one another!

This closeness often leads to "likeness." Aristotle said that a close friend is "another self." Have you ever noticed how close friends tend to walk the same, talk the same, like the same things, and finish one another's sentences? That's the consequence of spending a lot of "quality time" communicating with each other! It's almost as if they are formed into each other's image. What do you think would happen if you spent some serious quality time communicating with God in prayer?

One aspect of prayer is requesting "good things" from God. So what are the "good things" that we should request from him? First, it is normal and good to ask God for the necessities of our physical life, such as food, clothing, and shelter. It's also good to ask God's help with our everyday activities, whether at school, at work, at home, or on the ball field. Jesus told us to pray for such things, and he wants us to pray for them. But Jesus also told us to seek first the kingdom of God and his righteousness (see Mt 6:33). The most important things to pray for are those things that will help us to love as God loves and draw us closer to him. We need to ask God to help us

WORD TO THE WISE

One of the most powerful prayers, highly recommended by the Church and especially by Saint John Paul II (in fact, it was his favorite prayer) is the Rosary. The Rosary is a meditation on certain key moments in the lives of Jesus and Mary (called "mysteries"). Typically, praying one decade (a term that comes from the "ten" Hail Marys that are prayed) means meditating on one mystery. There are four sets of mysteries, with five mysteries in each set: the *Joyful Mysteries,* the *Luminous Mysteries,* the *Sorrowful Mysteries,* and the *Glorious Mysteries.* Learn how to pray this wonderful prayer by visiting www.usccb.org/prayer-and-worship/prayers-and-devotions/rosaries/how-to-pray-the-rosary.cfm or visit http://pauline.org/Rosary-with-Pope-Francis-App.

overcome temptation and sin in our lives. We need to ask God to help us to live by his new law of love. We need to ask God to help us be "pure in heart," as well as in body. God's word assures us that we will receive every grace we need: "Ask, and it will be given you" (Mt 7:7). But we need to ask. We need to pray.

THE SACRAMENTS

In addition to prayer, we also need to receive the sacraments. The sacraments are channels of God's grace to us. They are vehicles of the Holy Spirit. They enable us to share in God's own life and love so we can be his image in the world. They are powers that come forth from the heart of our mother, the Church, that strengthen our wills to choose what is good. Simply put, *the sacraments empower us to love as God loves, give the sincere gift of ourselves, and live as Jesus lived.*

In their classic definition, the "sacraments are efficacious signs of grace, instituted by Christ and entrusted to the Church, by which divine life is dispensed to us" (*CCC*, no. 1131). That's a mouthful! But it sounds more complicated than it really is. The key is understanding what a *sign* is.

A *sign* is something that "points to" a particular reality that is present. For example, a "danger" sign means you're *actually in* danger. Therefore, the sacraments as *signs* "point to" a particular reality that is present in each of them. But, there's also something unique about the sacraments as signs: they *actually make* particular realities from the past—particular moments in salvation history—present to us here and now. It's almost like we are somehow transported back to these moments (or these moments are somehow transported forward to us) and we get the chance to really "live through them" personally. We just looked at how this is the case with the sacrament of Baptism.

Another quality about signs is that they are perceptible by the senses. This point is important. Human beings need the sacraments because we are *body-persons*. Thus,

the sacraments are a testimony to how much God desires to be close to us! God meets us and comes to us through our bodies, through things we can see, hear, smell, taste, or touch—like water, oil, and bread and wine. That is, he comes to us through the material world. This is why the "visible sign" is often referred to as the "matter" of the sacrament.

Also, the sacraments always "do what they signify." That is, the sign is "efficacious" or produces certain results or "effects" in us. This is because Jesus works in and through them. By the water Jesus cleanses us from sin; by the oil he strengthens the gifts of the Spirit in our souls; and by the bread and wine he nourishes our souls and makes us "one body" with him. In other words, the "matter" *matters*!

In addition to the "matter" of the sacrament, there is the "form" of the sacrament. The form gives meaning to, or informs, the matter. In Baptism, for example, the matter is the water and the form is the words, "I baptize you in the name of the Father, and of the Son, and of the Holy Spirit."

Jesus established these signs during his life as special and powerful ways for us to share in his life and love (that is, as a means of grace), and so that he could be with us always, "until the end of time." By sharing in the life of the Son of God, we can live as sons and daughters of God. By sharing in the life of the new man, we can live as new men and women. By sharing in the love of *the* "image of God," we can love as God loves and be the images of God we were created to be. By sharing in the love of the "Bridegroom of the Church," we can give the sincere gift of ourselves in and through our bodies, be true "helpers" to one another, and live out God's *original plan* for life, love, marriage, and sex!

RECONCILIATION AND THE EUCHARIST: AS OFTEN AS WE NEED

In particular, we should make use of the grace available to us in the sacraments of Reconciliation and the Eucharist. Part of the beauty of these sacraments is that we can come to them as often as we need. And if we are serious about living out God's plan for us, we will need them often.

Frequently receiving the sacrament of Reconciliation is incredibly valuable. Not only do we receive the forgiveness of the sins we confess, we also receive the grace we will need to avoid those particular sins in the future. That's right—confession not only gets rid of our sins, it fills us with grace! So we should try to go regularly: once a month would be a good start. Of course, if we are aware of having committed a serious sin, we should go as soon as possible. But it's good to go on a regular basis, confessing even the little sins we commit every day. To give you an example, Saint Teresa of Calcutta and Saint John Paul II used to go to confession once a week. This was because they had such a great desire for holiness and purity that they noticed even the smallest ways (probably undetectable to us) in which they failed to love as God loves, and they wanted God to help them to love more perfectly. We should follow their lead.

FOR YOUR CONSIDERATION

Many parishes have set times for the sacrament of Reconciliation on Saturday afternoons, but you can also call your parish rectory and make an individual appointment.

Then we have the great gift of the Eucharist. What could be more important in living God's plan for life, love, marriage, and sex than to receive what Saint Thomas Aquinas called "the sacrament of love and pledge of love"?[9] In the Eucharist, Jesus desires to give the sincere gift of himself to us; he wants to give us his love. So, when we receive Jesus in the Eucharist, we receive his love into our souls. If our desire is to love as

Jesus loves, then receiving the Eucharist as often as we can is the surest and quickest way to do it.

Jesus knows we need him. He knows we need to be close to him if we are going to fulfill his great commandment of love. That's why at the Last Supper Jesus commanded his disciples to "Do this in remembrance of me" (Lk 22:19)—to celebrate the Eucharist regularly. The Church teaches that attending Mass every Sunday is how we honor these words of the Lord and "keep holy the Sabbath" (the third commandment). In addition to Sunday Mass, we can try to attend daily Mass as often as we can. We can also make a habit of stopping into a nearby church or chapel to visit Jesus in the Eucharist, for he is always waiting for us in the tabernacle. Some churches have special times for Eucharistic Adoration, which is when the Eucharist is placed into a beautiful case called a "monstrance" and set on the altar for people to worship. I have personally been deeply touched by the time I have spent in adoration. In these beautiful moments of intimacy with Jesus I have truly experienced his loving presence strengthening me.

WORKING AS IF EVERYTHING DEPENDS ON US

Again, prayer and the sacraments aren't magic. We need to do some work to prepare the "soil" of our hearts so that the grace we receive through prayer and the sacraments can take root and grow. And this work isn't for the fainthearted. We must "work as if everything depends on us" and "pray as if everything depends on

God." The real question is, "How badly do we want it?" Do we want the true happiness that only loving as God loves and giving the sincere gift of ourselves in and through our bodies can bring? If so, then we have to create a lifestyle that helps us do just that.

Maybe we will have to change some of the people we surround ourselves with and start walking with those who also want to live according to God's plan. Maybe we will have to find different social activities. Maybe we will have to change some of the movies or TV shows we watch, the books and magazines we read, the music we listen to, or the websites we view. Maybe we will have to radically transform our approach to dating relationships.

If we are willing to do our part, God will do his: we will grow and mature in our "new life" and more easily make the sincere gift of ourselves. Along the way, we should be patient with ourselves and not get too discouraged when we fall or fail. Growing and maturing is a process that takes time, is often slow, and tends to occur in spurts. I am still growing and maturing, and I fall and fail plenty! However, if we persevere, we have the assurance from God that we will become more and more the true "helpers" that he made husbands and wives to be for one another from "the beginning" and be an image and model of God's love in the world.

JOHN PAUL II
In His Own Words

The sacrament is a sign of grace, and it is *an efficacious sign*. It does not merely *indicate* and express grace in a visible way, in the manner of a sign, but *produces* grace and contributes efficaciously to cause that grace to become part of man and to *realize and fulfill the work of salvation* in him.

(TOB 87:5)

THINGS TO PONDER AND SHARE

1. Has there ever been a time in your life when you wished you could have a "do-over"? When and why?

2. What makes the redemption of human beings and the redemption of their bodies "good news"?

3. Try to find pictures of your Baptism day. Ask your parents about it. Who attended? What church was it held in? What were some of the gifts you received? Why did they choose your godparents? Ask your parents if they still have your baptismal gown, your "white

garment," and your baptismal candle. If possible, in-
terview your godparents. Ask them how they felt when
they were asked to take on that responsibility. How do
they understand their special role in your life?

4. If we in effect become "another Christ" in Baptism,
then we should live as Jesus lived. Search the Gospels
to find aspects of Jesus' life and character that you
want to imitate. Then create a "mission statement"
(a paragraph describing the sort of person you want
to be) for your life based on Jesus' life. Keep it where
you can read it every day as a reminder.

5. Define prayer in your own words. What are some
definitions offered in this chapter? How do you pray?

6. What is a sacrament? Do you see the sacraments as
important in your life? Why or why not? How can
the sacraments—particularly Reconciliation and the
Eucharist—help you to be more like Jesus?

7. What are some things in our lives that we may have
to change in order to more effectively live out God's
plan for life, love, marriage, and sex? Which of these
do you find most challenging and why?

·· READ THE CATECHISM OF THE CATHOLIC CHURCH ····

nos. 504–507, 519–521, 615–618, 1113–1130,
1262–1274, 1322–1332, 1422–1470, 1691, 1693–1696,
1701, 1708–1709, 1996–2000, 2626–2638, 2697–2719

CHAPTER 13

A MODEL MARRIAGE

Be subordinate to one another out of reverence for Christ. Wives should be subordinate to their husbands as to the Lord. . . . Husbands, love your wives, even as Christ loved the church and handed himself over for her. . . . This is a great mystery, but I speak in reference to Christ and the church.

—Ephesians 5:21–22, 25, 32 NAB

A SIGN OF CHRIST'S LOVE IN THE WORLD

In Anthony Doerr's Pulitzer Prize winning novel *All the Light We Cannot See*, a young girl named Marie-Laure goes blind when she is six years old. To help her cope with her blindness her father builds a perfect wooden model of their neighborhood so Marie-Laure can learn it by touch and always find her way home. Ultimately, this prepares her to fulfill her destiny of aiding the French resistance during World War II.

Is there a model for marriage that will always help us
find our way home to God and to follow his plan for us?
Is there a model that will help us to fulfill our destiny
of being "images of God" and prepare us for our roles
as wives and husbands, as mothers and fathers? Yes!
It is the marriage of Christ and the Church. This is the
"great mystery" that each and every Christian marriage
represents. This is the "model of love" that all Christian
husbands and wives are commanded and empowered to
learn from (see Mt 11:29; Jn 13:14–15). This is the "model
marriage"—and we can follow it because of the grace
that flows from the sacrament of Marriage.

It is commonly held that Jesus instituted the sacrament of Marriage at the wedding at Cana in Galilee,
where he performed his first miracle. Jesus' very presence at that wedding testifies to the goodness of marriage. And his celebrating the union of that Galilean
couple with good food and good drink testifies to the
joyfulness of the occasion (in fact, at a traditional Jewish
wedding the celebration could last for days). However,
these facts do not make marriage different than it had
been before. They simply affirm what marriage already
was: good and joyful. In order to raise marriage to new
and glorious heights, something would have to change.

Enter the Blessed Mother. Mary approached Jesus
with a potentially embarrassing situation for the newlyweds: the wine had run out. Jesus seems to answer her
concern harshly, saying, "O woman, what have you to do
with me? My hour has not yet come" (Jn 2:4). But Mary
takes no offense. She just instructs the servants, "Do

whatever he tells you" (Jn 2:5). Jesus then orders the servants to pour water into the stone jars that guests used for purification purposes (washing hands, feet, etc.). Let's just say as far as quality goes, this water couldn't compare with spring water from the Alps. Well, Jesus tells the servants to draw some out and bring it to the steward of the feast for him to taste. Could you imagine the terror that struck the servants at that very moment? They were probably thinking, "Bring the foot-washing water to the head steward to taste? Is this some kind of sick joke? We'll probably lose our jobs, not to mention get punished. We're going to be history—and all because of this Jesus from Nazareth!" They had no idea how right they were.

The response of the head steward must have shocked the servants: "This stuff is vintage! It is so generous of the newlyweds to save the best for last . . . and so unexpected, too." Imagine the servants standing there in amazement with gaping mouths as they thought, "Unexpected! You can say that again," and Jesus probably got a good laugh out of their reaction. I like to imagine that they started following the Lord that very day.

> **FOR YOUR CONSIDERATION**
>
> We can also see here that Mary is the "New Eve," since Eve was called "woman" by Adam.

When Jesus changed the water into wine, he also changed "ordinary" marriage into something *extraordinary.* He made what had always been quite a *natural* thing for a man and woman to do—get married and raise a family—into a *supernatural* thing for a man and woman to do. At Cana in Galilee Jesus identified the marriage of his followers with *his own marriage with the Church*—a marriage that would ultimately take place on the Cross at Calvary.

Look carefully and notice the imagery in the story. Jesus calls Mary "woman," just like he does when he's on the Cross: "Woman, behold, your son!" (Jn 19:26). Jesus refers to his "hour," which in John's Gospel always means the hour of his passion and death. And Jesus changes the water into wine, which prefigures the blood and water that flowed from his side and gave life to the Church.

Did U Know

While the marriage of two non-Christians or a Christian and a non-Christian may be considered good and natural, only the marriage of a baptized man and a baptized woman is sacramental.

The marriage of Christ and the Church on the Cross is made present all over again when a baptized man and woman get married. The grace that flows from Christ's giving of himself in and through his body for his Bride, the Church, enables Christian spouses to do the same through the sacrament of Marriage. Because of this outpouring of grace, Jesus can command his followers to live out God's plan for marriage from "the beginning."

They have become new men and women in Baptism, "remade" in the image of Jesus Christ, and therefore as spouses are to be *the physical image of the Trinity* and *the physical representation of Christ's love for the Church* in the world. And the sacrament of Marriage makes all this possible.

JESUS CONFIRMS AND RENEWS GOD'S ORIGINAL PLAN FOR MARRIAGE

Let's sum up the Creator's original plan for marriage, and show how Jesus, in his marriage to the Church, confirms it and renews it as the model that *all Christian marriages* must follow.

Marriage is the *sincere gift of self* of a man and woman to one another and *a pledge to love one another every day as God loves*: "Love is patient and kind . . ." As such, marriage is a *free and conscious choice* to give one's whole self for the true good of the other. By this gift of their whole selves, *which includes the gift of their whole lives*, the man and woman *belong exclusively* to each other. They establish a *covenant* before God saying, "I am yours, and you are mine." Thus, the marriage of the man and woman is *initiated* or *established* by means of the *mutual consent* of the couple, which is expressed in their *spoken vows* before God. However, the marriage is *completed* or *accomplished* (often referred to as *consummated*) and the marriage covenant *ratified* by means of sexual union. The sexual union of the man and woman embodies their spoken vows: they give *themselves* totally to one another by giving *their bod-ies* totally to one another. It is through this *bodily union after their spoken vows* (which is a true communion of persons) that the Holy Spirit joins the spouses together in a bond that is *indissoluble* and *permanent*. And this sincere gift of self of the spouses to one another in and through their bodies in sexual union opens itself up to the gift of the child. Since marriage is an image of the life-giving communion of persons of the Trinity, it is by nature directed toward the *procreation and education of children*, and must always remain *open to the trans-mission of life*.

Jesus gives the free and conscious gift of himself for his Bride, the Church. He said, "No one takes [my life] from me, but I lay it down of my own accord" (Jn 10:18). Jesus also gives his whole self for her good: he "emptied him-self, taking the form of a servant" (Phil 2:7). He pledges to love us every day (Jer 31:3; Ps 136:1; Rom 5:8), and his love is perfect, expressing all the features of love: "Love is patient and kind. . . ." Jesus shed his blood as a sign of the "new and everlast-ing covenant," accomplishing in his body what he had initiated in the vows he had made to Israel, namely, that he would be hers and she would be his (see Ex 6:7–8).

NOTABLE QUOTABLE

The Church living with Christ who lives forever may never be divorced from him.

—Saint Augustine

When Jesus gives his body to his Bride, he becomes "one body" with her, and is permanently bound to her by the Holy Spirit (see Jn 19:30). And Jesus' gift of self gives life: "I came that they may have life, and have it abundantly" (Jn 10:10). In fact, Jesus *is* life (Jn 14:6). His communion with the Church gives life to "children of God" in Baptism and educates them in the way of his commandments (Mt 28:19–20). And as much as Jesus' love is universal, it is also exclusive. Saint Augustine once said that Jesus loves "each of us as if there were only us" and would have climbed on the cross if each of us were the *only* one to save.

So when a baptized man and woman get married, they are

> Read 1 Corinthians 13:4–8:
>
> "Love is patient and kind . . ." Then read it again and substitute "Jesus" for the word "love." See how it works perfectly! Now, read it a third time and substitute your own name for the word "love." See how this works . . . well . . . let's just say, not quite as perfectly. This exercise is a great "examination of conscience" that can help us to see where we need to love better. Try it before the next time you go to confession or at night before you go to bed as a review of your day.

declaring that they accept God's original plan for marriage, confirmed and renewed by Jesus Christ, and are committed to living according to this plan. This is the meaning of Saint Paul's exhortation to Christian spouses to "be subordinate to one another out of reverence for Christ" (Eph 5:21). And this is why at a wedding the couple declares their consent to what God has revealed to the Church *about* marriage before they give themselves to one another *in* marriage. They must testify that they know and understand, at least on a basic level, what they are getting into. The couple does this by answering these three questions that the Church asks them through her "official witness," the priest or deacon:

> *N. and N., have you come here to enter into Marriage without coercion,*
> *freely and wholeheartedly?*
>
> *Are you prepared, as you follow the path of Marriage, to love and honor each other*
> *for as long as you both shall live?*
>
> *Are you prepared to accept children lovingly from God and to bring them up*
> *according to the law of Christ and his Church?*

And the answer must be a resounding, "Yes! We will."

A YES WITH MEANING

I say a *resounding* "yes" for a few practical reasons. As already mentioned, by declaring their consent, the man and woman are saying that they understand what they are getting into when they enter marriage. Well, by their "yes," the man and woman are also saying that they are *free* and *able* to enter marriage (e.g., that they aren't already married, among other things). In fact, when the priest or deacon used to say, "If there is anyone present who knows why these two should not be joined in holy matrimony, let him speak now or forever hold his peace," he was really asking an honest question about the freedom of the man and woman to marry. The romanticized scene where another man bursts into the church out of breath at that very moment, saying, "Because I'm in love with her!" really has nothing to do with the question. If he said, "Because I'm married to her," *that* would be an issue.

A resounding "yes" is necessary as well because by it the man and woman are saying that they have *no reservations* regarding their marriage. This means that they are not withholding necessary and important information from each other that could seriously impact the other's choice of marriage. It also means that they are not placing any conditions on their promises, such as: "I will love and honor you as my husband unless you do this," or "I will love and honor you as my wife unless this happens." That's why the Church has always held that prenuptial agreements contradict what marriage is and that the couple who enters into one cannot enter into marriage. Marriage is permanent and unconditional.

If for any reason the couple cannot answer a resounding "yes," then their marriage will not be *valid*. If their marriage is not valid, then they are not "lawfully" or truly married according to Christ and the Church. Experience shows that often the man and woman may not become fully aware that their "yes" wasn't genuine until years later. This is why the Church recognizes annulments, but not divorce.

You may be wondering exactly what the difference is between an annulment and a divorce. It can be very confusing. Basically, if the man and the woman *are not* validly married, this can be recognized by the Church in what is called a "decree of nullity" or annulment. An annulment isn't a "Catholic divorce," nor is it something that the Church "gives" to the couple. Rather, it is something that the Church *declares* to be the case: that the couple was never truly married in the first place. Hence, once they receive an annulment, both the man and woman would be free to marry someone else.

On the other hand, a divorce implies that there was indeed a marriage, but that it has been "broken," causing the man and woman to no longer be bound to one another. However, since God has revealed that in a valid marriage the Holy Spirit permanently binds the man and woman to one another (just as he binds the Father to the Son and Christ to the Church), the Church states that divorce is *impossible*. Therefore, if a man and woman *are* validly married, and then get divorced and marry someone else, they are committing adultery. This is the meaning of Jesus' words: "Whoever divorces his wife (unless the marriage is unlawful) and marries another commits adultery" (Mt 19:9 NAB).

Christ's words on divorce and remarriage are clear and direct. We know, however, that these situations can be very complicated and complex. Life is messy and people are wounded. And so, while those who have entered a new union without an annulment are living in an objective situation not in keeping with God's plan, we should always refrain from judging the people themselves. Only God knows the depths of their hearts and consciences. The Church, for her part, is seeking ways to reach out to these couples. In her great love, the Church seeks to accompany them, to lead them to a fuller realization of God's plan for marriage in their lives, and to draw them more fully into the life of the community. And it is this same great love that compels the Church to be unwavering in upholding the teaching she has received from Jesus about the indissolubility of marriage. It is a teaching that is good news and desperately needed in our world today, and is the only way to the joy that Jesus desires for us (see Jn 15:11).

VOWS THAT MAKE A MARRIAGE

Once the couple has declared that they accept and are committing themselves to what God has revealed to his Church about marriage and are entering into a valid marriage, they can go on to declare their consent to each other. It is here that the couple "confers" the sacrament of Marriage on each other. Contrary to popular belief, in the Roman Catholic Church the priest or deacon doesn't "marry" the couple. He *witnesses*, as an official representative of the Church, the man and the woman "marrying each other."

So, if the man and woman give the sacrament of Marriage to each other, what is the efficacious sign of the sacrament? The simple answer is *the marriage vows*. However, these vows are actually expressed in two ways: through spoken language (spoken vows or "consent") and through body language (sexual union or "consummation"). You could say that in order for a marriage to take place, the man and woman must speak two languages. "Their consent and their bodily union are the divinely appointed means whereby they become 'one flesh'" (*The Joy of Love*, no. 75). The mutual consent culminating and expressed in the spoken vows is a promise to become "one flesh" and all that this means, and a sign of the marriage being initiated or established. Sexual union is the couple becoming "one flesh" through the union of their bodies and a sign of the marriage being completed. The consent expressed through the spoken vows is the *form* of the sacrament. These vows *inform* and "give meaning to the sexual relationship and free it from ambiguity" (*The Joy of Love*, no. 74). More on that in the next chapter! (No skipping ahead . . . .)

If you have ever been to a wedding, I'm sure you have heard the spoken vows before: *I take you to be my lawful wife/husband, to have and to hold, from this day forward, for better, for worse, for richer, for poorer, in sickness and in health, until death do us part.* These words are a solemn promise by the spouses to give the sincere gift of their whole selves to one another, which includes the gift of their whole lives, and to love each other as God loves every day, displaying the features of love discussed in Chapter 3: "Love is patient and kind. . . ."

After the man and woman exchange their consent through their spoken vows, they exchange rings. These rings are not *efficacious signs*, but they are signs nonetheless. They "point to a reality that is present": the marriage of the couple enacted by the vows they exchanged. Yet, it is important to note that it is by their consent that the man and woman are married, not by the rings. That's why in a Catholic marriage the man and woman do not say, "With this ring I thee wed," but, "Receive this ring, as a sign of my love and fidelity. In the name of the Father, and of the Son, and of the Holy Spirit."

At the very moment when the man and the woman give the sincere gift of their whole selves to one another in their vows, their relationship undergoes a transformation. Now they "belong" to each other. Now they are spouses. God then blesses this "exchange of persons" and "mutual belonging" through his representative, the priest or deacon. That is why it is at this point and only at this point that God's representative pronounces the couple "man and wife."

He then says the much anticipated words: "You may kiss the bride." Now, you may be tempted to think that since the deal has been "sealed with a kiss," that's the end. But while the marriage has been *initiated*, it hasn't been *accomplished*. The sacrament of Marriage has been *conferred*, but it hasn't been *completed*. As mentioned above, to become "one flesh," *the man and the woman will actually need to become one flesh.*

That is, they are going to have to speak a second language.

JOHN PAUL II
In His Own Words

Marriage as a sacrament is contracted by means of *the word*, . . . "I take you as my wife / as my husband." . . . [However, it] can only be fulfilled by . . . conjugal [marital] intercourse.

(TOB 103:2)

Thus, *from the words* with which the man and the woman express their readiness to become "one flesh" . . . we pass *to the reality* that corresponds to these words. Both the one and the other element are important *with regard to the structure of the sacramental sign.*

(TOB 103:3)

THINGS TO PONDER AND SHARE

1. Before people build a house or a building, they usually make a model. What is the purpose of having a model?

2. Have you ever experienced God changing water into wine in your life: making what is ordinary into something extraordinary? Explain the situation.

3. How does the marriage of Christians represent the marriage of Christ and the Church? What are some ways that Christian spouses can love one another as Christ loves the Church?

4. Why is it so important for anyone seeking marriage to understand and accept God's plan for marriage from "the beginning"? Why is it so important that they are *able* to understand and *freely* accept it?

5. In the sacrament of Marriage, words transform the relationship. Have you ever experienced the power of words to transform a relationship in your life, for better or for worse? When and how?

6. Why is it significant that a man and a woman belong to each other only when they become spouses?

READ THE CATECHISM OF THE CATHOLIC CHURCH

nos. 1601, 1613, 1615–1617, 1625–1632, 1643–1651, 2382–2391

CHAPTER 14

BODY LANGUAGE

The body, however, is not for [sexual] immorality, but for the Lord, and the Lord is for the body. . . . Avoid [sexual] immorality. Every other sin a person commits is outside the body, but the [sexually] immoral person sins against his own body. Do you not know that your body is a temple of the holy Spirit within you, whom you have from God, and that you are not your own? For you have been purchased at a price. Therefore, glorify God in your body.

—1 Corinthians 6:13b, 18–20 NAB

SEX THAT TELLS THE TRUTH

I'm sure you have heard the phrase "actions speak louder than words." It's a clever and concise way of saying that our body language and our spoken language need to "say" the same thing. Our body language is often "louder" because it can either fulfill or contradict what our words have said. We can see this most vividly in the "language of the body" spoken by a man and a woman in sexual union.

Before we go on, however, we need to ask ourselves a question: What is the purpose of language in the first place? It's communication, of course. Communication is extremely important. Remember how from "the beginning" human beings were created in the image of the Trinity *as persons* for a *communion of persons*? It would be pretty difficult to form a communion of persons if we couldn't communicate with each other. So you could say that *language helps us to fulfill the purpose of our existence*! Actually, only a certain kind of language does: one that *communicates truth*.

It's only when two persons give a gift of themselves that is *sincere*, that is, *what is truly good* for each other, that they "become one" with each other. A "communion of persons" based on lies and falsehood wouldn't be a communion at all. This is why *truth-telling is an essential part of being human*: we can't love as God loves and form a communion of persons without being truthful. And since we are body-persons created in the image of God, we must "tell *the* truth"—which is *God's* truth, not *my* truth or *your* truth—with our words *and* with our bodies.

But what is *the truth* that the "language of the body" is supposed to "tell" in the sexual union of a man and a woman? It's supposed to say, "I am yours and you are mine!" Right from "the beginning," sexual union was meant to express mutual belonging and communicate the sincere gift of the spouses' whole selves to one another. In the last chapter we learned that a man and woman only "belong" to each other *after* they exchange vows and those vows are blessed by God through his representative, the priest or deacon. This is because when a couple exchanges their vows they are in fact exchanging their persons. Only spouses belong to each other, for only they have given the sincere gift of their whole selves to one another. That sincere gift includes the gift of their bodies, because *they are* their bodies. And because only spouses belong to each other, only they have the right to express their love for each other in a sexual way (see 1 Cor 7:3–4). This means that *all sexual relations, and not just sexual intercourse, belong exclusively to married persons*. This is actually the full sense of the sixth commandment, "You shall not commit adultery." This commandment is more properly understood as prohibiting sexual relations with anyone who is not your spouse—that is, with anyone who does not belong to you and to whom you do not belong. Therefore, the "language of the body" in sexual union can only "tell the truth" *if the man and woman are spouses.*

In addition, sex is supposed to be *the marriage vows communicated in body language.* The words of the spoken vows—"I give the sincere gift of my whole self to you in and through my body. I desire to be one with you and form a life-giving communion of persons"—are fulfilled in the sexual union of the spouses. The "sign" of the sacrament of Marriage is complete only when the marriage vows have been expressed in both spoken language and body language. And since the sacraments always "do what they signify," when a baptized man and woman become "one flesh" (sometimes translated "one body") in sexual union, *they actually become "one flesh."* It is through their first sexual union after their spoken vows have been blessed by God and his Church that the Holy Spirit joins the man and woman in a permanent and unbreakable bond (often called an *indissoluble* bond). As it turns out, *the spouses themselves* (in and through *their bodies*) are the *matter* of the sacrament.

And this is precisely why sexual union completes and accomplishes (that is, *consummates*) the marriage.

You may recall that signs point to a reality that is present (e.g., a "danger" sign means you are in danger), but the sacraments as signs actually *make* certain realities present. So how does that apply to the sexual union of Christian spouses? What realities are made present by their sexual union?

In God's original plan for marriage and sex, the sexual union of spouses was a clear image of the life-giving communion of Persons within the Trinity. After sin, with our human nature being "out of order" and our capacity to love as God loves seriously impacted, sexual union lost this clarity. But through the death and resurrection of Jesus Christ and his gift of the Spirit of love received in Baptism, the communion of Christian spouses in sexual union has been restored as a sign of the communion of Persons within the Trinity.

In Christ, the communion of spouses also receives a new significance: it represents the "holy communion" of Christ and his Bride, the Church. This communion was supremely expressed when he gave the sincere gift of his whole self in and through his body on the Cross. On the Cross, Jesus accomplished or "consummated" his marriage with the Church, and he memorializes and renews it in the Eucharist. Becoming "one body" with the Lord in Holy Communion strengthens our bond with Christ and imparts grace to us for living the Christian life. Similarly, each and every sexual communion between Christian spouses, after the one that consummates their marriage, memorializes and renews their marriage. Becoming "one body" in sexual communion strengthens the bond between the spouses and imparts grace to them for living the Christian married life. That's right . . . for Christian spouses, sex is a means of God's grace!

SEX THAT'S SIGNIFICANT AND SINCERE

It should be clear that in order for the body language of sexual union to tell "the truth," it must be *between a man and a woman who are spouses* and it must *express God's love, that is, the sincere gift of self.* It must truly embody what marriage is: a sign of the communion of

Persons within the Trinity, and the love of Christ for the Church. You could say that from the "beginning" sex was supposed to be *significant*! The sexual union of spouses can only be significant if it exemplifies God's love. But even more, it can only be sincere if it genuinely communicates the spoken vows that give the sexual relationship its meaning.

Now, certain acts do this well, and others do not. Some acts communicate God's love as expressed through the spoken vows, and others contradict it. Some sexual acts correspond to God's plan for us, and others oppose that plan. To recognize the difference, it may be helpful to recap briefly what God's plan for life, love, marriage, and sex is.

We have learned that man and woman are created in the image of God to love as God loves in and through their bodies. We defined that love as "the sincere gift of self." That kind of love is really about the other person and what is *truly good* for him or her, as well as a free choice to give oneself for the other. Since true love is self-giving, the greatness of the love is determined by the amount one is willing to give of oneself. Marriage is the gift of one's whole self, which includes the gift of one's whole life, and this is what makes married love such a radical example of God's love in the world. This total gift of the man and woman to one another in marriage is embodied in the total gift of their bodies in sexual union, since the person is his or her body. Additionally, by the sincere and total gift of the man and woman to one another in and through their bodies they image God as Trinity, a life-giving communion of Persons. The total gift of the spouses to one another in sexual union opens itself up to the gift of the child. As the original blessing of the Creator upon the first married couple (and every married couple that would follow them), fruitfulness is a responsibility built into the nature and mission of marriage itself.

With this in mind, let's see if we can recognize the difference between sexual acts that correspond to God's plan for us, and therefore are significant and sincere, and those that do not and are not.

EXCLUSIVELY FOR HUSBAND AND WIFE

First, for sex to correspond to God's plan, to be a sign of the communion of Persons within the Trinity and the love of Christ for the Church, and to embody the sincere gift of the man and woman's whole selves to one another, the man and the woman *must actually be married.* As we have discussed, through their spoken vows the man and woman give their whole selves to one another in the marriage covenant. They effectively say, "I am yours and you are mine." It is only by those vows that they belong to one another and have the right to express that love in a sexual way. And as we said, this goes for all sexual relations, not just sexual intercourse. With this in mind, we can see why premarital sex is clearly against God's plan for life, love, marriage, and sex. We can also see why it is wrong for those who are engaged to be married to "engage" in sexual relations.

Since the engaged to be married *aren't married*, their sexual union cannot be sincere. They would be saying with their bodies, "I am yours; I belong to you," but that wouldn't be the truth, since they haven't exchanged their persons by exchanging their vows. Their sexual union cannot express, memorialize, or renew marriage vows that haven't been made! An engaged couple may love each other, but they do not "belong" to each other. Not yet, anyway. Perhaps an analogy might help. The president-elect is the person who is going to become the president, but isn't yet the president. The president-elect only actually becomes the president and has the powers of that office when he or she takes the oath of office. And this oath (or vow) must follow a certain form or the president-elect doesn't become the president.

Once the man and woman do exchange vows and belong to each other, their sexual union must express the *exclusivity* of these vows. Sex must say, "It's you and only you! I am totally yours. I belong to you alone." It should also be obvious, then, how adultery is so clearly opposed to the exclusivity that sexual union is meant to communicate and a grave violation of God's plan for life, love, marriage, and sex. This also helps to explain why so-called "open" relationships (polyamory), as well as polygamy (marriage to more than one person at the same time), find no part in God's plan. You cannot give the gift of your whole self to more than one person! God created sex as the embodiment of the sincere gift of the man and woman's whole selves to one another, to be for the two of them alone.

This exclusivity goes for our minds and hearts as well. Jesus said, "Everyone who looks at a woman lustfully has already committed adultery with her in his heart" (Mt 5:28). If someone has lust for a person who is not their spouse, they clearly wouldn't be giving their mind and heart totally to their spouse, which is what they promise in their marriage vows. They also would be reducing the other woman or man to an object and wouldn't be seeing them as a person created by God for her or his own sake. Sadly, such lusting has become part of the cultural fabric with Internet pornography becoming so pervasive and socially accepted.

It should be clear how porn utterly contradicts God's plan. The people depicted are obviously violating God's plan on multiple levels. The viewers see them merely as objects of sexual pleasure and

FOR YOUR CONSIDERATION

Helps to Break Free from Porn Use:

1. Make a firm decision to stop, and delete all pornographic websites and images from your devices.

2. Obtain a server level Internet filter, and only use technology in common areas (not in private).

3. Identify the situations and feelings that lead you to look. Develop ways to avoid those situations and find healthy outlets for those feelings.

4. Find support from a friend who shares your values.

5. Speak to a parent or other trusted adult.

6. Get spiritual advice from a priest or a religious brother or sister.

7. Receive the sacraments of Reconciliation and Eucharist often.

8. Pray hard, asking the Blessed Mother and the saints to help you with their prayers too!

not as persons created in the image of God. Tragically, the "actors" are often supporting drug addictions or may even be victims of human trafficking. So, people who support the porn industry through their viewing are promoting social injustice by encouraging sexual immorality and exploitation, drug cartels, and sex trafficking. Studies show that viewing pornography is addictive and impacts brain chemistry in a way similar to other addictions. (This doesn't take a study, however: anyone who is hooked on porn knows that it seems practically impossible not to "point and click.") Porn sets up unrealistic expectations about sex. These expectations lead people to more and more sexually deviant behaviors, and to feel as if they need to replicate a porn video in order to "compete" with the porn itself or be sexually desirable at all. It is being shown that regular porn use can lead to sexual dysfunction in men at younger ages, as well as to an inability to build real emotional bonds and healthy relationships in men and women alike. In other words,

Did U Know

One hopeful sign is that countries are beginning to make stricter laws regulating Internet porn sites to try to keep children safe, and pornography is even being examined by some states and countries for its impact on public health. For the details on these facts and to hear the heartbreaking stories of those whose lives and relationships have been negatively impacted by pornography, see www.fightthenewdrug.org.

virtual sex leads to problems in *real relationships*. With eleven being the average age of first exposure to pornography and people (especially young men) growing up on a steady diet of porn, who can doubt that porn is a contributing factor to the increase in sexual aggression and sexual assaults?

But we can see hopeful signs, however. The dangers and detriments of viewing pornography are beginning to be publicly admitted and recognized, as more studies are done and more people tell their stories.

EXCLUSIVELY FOR MAN AND WOMAN

In God's plan for creation, as we have just discussed, marriage and sex are exclusively for a husband and a wife. This also means that in God's plan for creation, marriage and sex are *exclusively for a man and a woman*. Only a man and a woman can become "one flesh" and form a *life-giving communion of persons* through sexual union. From "the beginning," sexual difference is not something *accidental* to marriage, but rather something *essential* to marriage (see Chapter 6). Only the bodies of a man and a woman are made for union with each other. Only they have complementary reproductive systems and organs that, when joined together, form one biological unit that is, by its nature, capable of procreation. The unitive (spousal) and procreative (generative) meanings of the body were stamped by God right into its very structure. In "the beginning" the first man and woman clearly perceived these meanings. Thus, two persons of the same sex cannot become "one body" or form a genuine communion of persons in and through their bodies by engaging in homosexual acts. Their bodies were not made for union with each other. This helps to explain why it is impossible for two persons of the same sex to be spouses. They cannot become "one flesh" in marriage because they cannot become "one flesh" in sexual union and because their sexual acts, *by their very nature*, can never be life-giving and open to the gift of the child, the "third" sprung from them both.

CHECK IT OUT

Ministries like Courage (https://couragerc.org) assist men and women with same-sex attractions in living chaste lives.

It must be emphatically stated that this aspect of God's plan in no way means that those who experience homosexual feelings or same sex-attraction shouldn't be treated with love and kindness. Of course they should—they are *persons*! Every sign of unjust discrimination must be carefully avoided, and any form of aggression or violence strongly condemned (*The Joy of Love*, no. 250). Neither does this truth of God's plan for love, marriage, and sex indicate that such feelings are in themselves sinful, even if they aren't in tune with God's plan for creation. Those who wrestle with these feelings deserve our compassion and respect, not our judgment, as Pope Francis has reminded us. However, it does explain why *homosexual acts* and "same-sex marriage" contradict the very meaning and purpose of marriage as a sign of the Trinity and of Christ's union with the Church, as well as why "there are absolutely no grounds for considering homosexual unions to be in any way similar or even remotely analogous to God's plan for marriage and family" (*The Joy of Love*, no. 251). Those who engage in homosexual acts cannot give the sincere gift of their whole selves to one another in and through their bodies and form a life-giving communion of persons. Jesus himself affirmed that God's plan from "the beginning" was for marriage to be between one man and one woman when he said, "Have you not read that from the beginning the Creator '*made them male and female*' . . . and '*the two shall become one flesh*'?" (Mt 19:4–5 NAB).

> **Did U Know**
>
> This point about how only a man and a woman can become "one body" because of their complementary reproductive systems is emphasized by Robert P. George in his article: "What Marriage Is and Isn't" (http://www.firstthings.com/article/2009/08/what-marriage-is-and-what-it-isnt). George is the McCormick Professor of Jurisprudence at Princeton University.

A FREE AND CONSCIOUS CHOICE

Just as the sincere gift of one's whole self in the spoken vows must be a free and conscious choice, so must the sincere gift of one's whole self in sexual union. Sex cannot be forced upon someone. This is called rape—and it is a horrific violation of a person's dignity. Statistics show that one in five women will be raped in their lifetime and one in ten will be raped by an intimate partner (even her husband).[10] "Rape" here means forced intercourse, attempted forced intercourse, or alcohol/drug facilitated intercourse. Sexual violence on college campuses is a growing problem that has been receiving public attention. Sadly, rape is the most underreported crime. It should go without saying that a person who has been violated in this way bears no moral fault. Sadly, so many rape victims blame themselves for something *they didn't do* but that was *done to them*.

Because sexual union should be a free and conscious choice, a person cannot be manipulated or tricked into sexual relations. This can happen when one person puts pressure on the other, or tries to manipulate the person through guilt, or lies to him or her. It can also happen when a person tries to get the other to drink alcohol or take drugs so they are "more willing" to have sex. In truth, this makes the person "less willing," because alcohol and drugs severely compromise their ability to will anything—to make a free and conscious choice. (Notice that this is true whether their partner tries to get them into that state or they are already in that state.)

Sex also is not freely chosen when it is simply the result of sexual instincts or drives. Genesis 4:1 describes sexual union between the man and woman as "knowledge" ("Adam knew his wife Eve"). So Saint John Paul II stated that sex is raised to the level of the person involving a free and conscious choice, and is not the result of mere sexual reactivity as is the case with other animals. While people are more "in the mood" at certain times, to have sex solely in response to the body's impulses resembles the way animals behave as opposed to the way humans should behave as body-persons. To act only from drives would amount to the man and the woman using one another to fulfill their sexual urges, which is anything but love.

A SINCERE GIVING

In their spoken vows the man and woman give the sincere gift of their whole selves to one another, so their sexual union must communicate a sincere giving. The man and woman give their minds, their hearts, and their lives to each other, and all of this is communicated through their bodily union. In sexual union, the husband and wife should be focused on each other and not primarily on themselves. In this way, their mutual giving and receiving spring from self-giving as its source. This natural dynamic of giving and receiving pleasure as the spouses give themselves sincerely to one another is *very good* and is *a gift from God* to spouses! The spouses "speak" the language of "sincere gift" "through gestures and reactions, through the whole . . . dynamism of tension and enjoyment—whose direct source is the body in its masculinity and femininity" (TOB 123:4). Yes, in God's plan sex is supposed to be a source of joy and enjoyment for the spouses!

However, even in marriage, sex can become self-centered and sought exclusively for the pleasure it gives. In this case, it becomes about taking rather than genuinely giving. This can happen, for example, when lust is the motivation for sex. As we have previously discussed, lust leads us to view each other as *simply bodies*, as objects to be used for our own purposes. While love helps us see the other as a person—someone created in the image of God for his or her own sake, and revealed in and through their body—lust inclines us to depersonalize others. Love says, "I *give myself* for *your* own sake." Lust says, "I *take you* for *my* own sake." If someone has lust for their spouse, they view him or her as an object for their own sexual gratification. A person can even begin to treat his or her spouse simply as a means of sexual enjoyment. In this case, sex becomes a source of alienation and not communion in the relationship. It should be clear that such attitudes and actions do not embody a sincere giving of one's whole self.

This is one of the problems with masturbation, which is "the deliberate stimulation of the genital organs in order to derive sexual pleasure" (*CCC*, no. 2352). Such an act is completely self-centered and actually fosters a general disposition of self-absorption. But "love refuses every impulse to close in on itself" (*The Joy of Love*, no. 80). Since sex is supposed to be a sincere giving of oneself to another, masturbation is opposed to God's plan for our sexuality. Also, lustful thoughts, which Jesus condemns, often inspire and accompany such acts.

Sexual feelings and sexual pleasure are *very good* since God created them. He created the sexual urge as part of the dynamism that leads us to seek communion and sexual pleasure to be enjoyed within marriage. However, when we make a deliberate choice to allow our imagination to run wild or to seek sexual pleasure for itself, apart from the sincere gift of one's whole self, we inevitably turn others into sexual objects and distort God's plan. Masturbation encourages the impulse to close in on oneself instead of embodying a sincere giving of oneself. Such acts also do not open up to the new life that can spring from a communion of persons in sexual union.

This said, while someone who falls into this sin or has developed this habit should take it seriously and try to break from it, many factors (and not only lust) can influence such acts, and the Lord understands them all. And so, do not be overwhelmingly ashamed, give up hope, or feel as if you are a terrible person altogether worthy of hell. Try to identify your triggers and what is motivating you besides mere sexual feelings (e.g., stress, frustration, loneliness, poor self-image), as well as recognize patterns so you can break them (e.g., you may be more prone at a particular time or in a particular place). If you are looking at images that encourage lustful thoughts, like Internet porn, you obviously should do what you can to stop (see the sidebar "Helps to Break Free from Porn Use" on page 149). Perhaps speak to a priest or religious brother or sister for spiritual advice, support, and guidance. Pray for God's help in all of this, and seek his grace in the sacraments, especially the sacrament of Reconciliation. But above all, remember God loves you and that his mercy "spurs us on to do our best" (Pope Francis, *The Joy of the Gospel*, no. 44).

A GIFT THAT GIVES LIFE

When a couple declares their mutual consent to give the sincere gift of their whole selves to one another and pledges to love each other as God loves, they make a solemn promise to "accept children lovingly as from God." This is because marriage, as an image of the Trinity, is a *life-giving communion of persons*. The man and woman's total gift of themselves in and through their bodies in sexual union opens itself up to the gift of the child. Marriage is also a sign of the love of Christ for the Church, for Jesus came to give life abundantly, make us sons and daughters of God, and expand God's family. The prevailing attitude between the spouses ought to be one of generosity and hospitality—the child is a gift from God to be accepted and welcomed with open hearts and open arms.

In addition to the body's *spousal* or *unitive meaning*, its capacity to express love and communion, it has a *procreative* or *generative meaning*, its capacity to give life. And so, the sexual union of spouses must retain both meanings. The "language of the body" in the sexual union of a man and a woman is not only supposed to say, "I am yours and you are mine," but also "I may be a father/I may be a mother." Both the unitive and pro-creative meanings are essential to sex as God created it. That is why the Church teaches that "each and every marital act must of necessity retain its intrinsic rela-tionship to the procreation of human life" (Blessed Paul VI, *Of Human Life*, no. 11). The child "'does not come from outside as something added on to the mutual love of the spouses, but springs from the very heart of that mutual giving, as its fruit and fulfillment' . . . [and] is present from the beginning of love as an essential fea-ture, one that cannot be denied without disfiguring that love itself" (*The Joy of Love*, no. 80, quoting *CCC*, no. 2366). The word *matrimony* (marriage) comes from the Latin root *mater, matris* (mother). Marriage and moth-erhood (and of course fatherhood, by implication) are intrinsically intertwined in the "logic" of love.

And so, in order for the procreative meaning of the body and sex to be respected and preserved, "no gen-ital act of husband and wife can refuse this meaning, even when, for various reasons, it may not always in fact beget a new life" (*The Joy of Love*, no. 80). That is, the spouses must never do anything that *directly and intentionally causes* any sexual act to be infertile, which includes "any action which either before, at the moment of, or after sexual intercourse, is specifically intended to prevent procreation" (Blessed Paul VI, *Of Human Life*, no. 14). This is why the Church has consistently taught that, in addition to direct and elective sterilization, contraception, whatever the form (e.g., pill, patch, condom, withdrawal), is opposed to God's plan for life, love, marriage, and sex.

There are many reasons couples choose to use contraception, and these reasons aren't always wrong, even if the choice to use contraception is. Couples are often simply afraid or doubt that they will be able to care for another child. And so we should have compassion regarding the situations these couples face. At the same time we should be clear that the use of contraception "contradicts" the language of the body, which is supposed to be communicated in the sexual union of a man and woman and breaks the solemn promises made when the couple declared their mutual consent. By depriving sexual union of its procreative capacity a couple that uses contraception deprives sexual union of its full truth. So their union ceases to be an act of true love (see TOB 123:6) or form a true communion of persons. By directly and intentionally preventing their love from giving life, they are disfiguring their union as an image of the Trinity and the love of Christ for the Church. And by refusing to be "pro" God's creation, they are in effect saying to God, "We are the lords and givers of life, not you." And they say to each other, "I do not really want to become 'one flesh' with you." Not only that, they actually might be killing their own flesh.

CONTRACEPTION OR ABORTION?

Most chemical "contraceptives," like birth control pills, contraceptive patches, or injections, act as *abortifacients*.[11] That means that they can cause a very early abortion. They usually do this by disrupting the uterine lining so that the newly conceived human being cannot be implanted in the womb. This is a "backup plan" built into these drugs, just in case they fail to work in their contraceptive capacity. When you consider the number of women who use chemical "contraceptives," and that at least sometimes they act as abortifacients, it's almost mind-boggling to think about how many babies really die every year by abortion, since about 1.1 million surgical abortions are performed in the United States[12] and over 50 million are performed worldwide *every year*. It is tragic that most people are not aware of or informed about this aspect of chemical contraceptives. I believe many would make a different choice about using them if they knew.

It's important to remember that the *fundamental task* of marriage is to serve life. Children are always a blessing and never a burden. They are not a disease to be eradicated by taking a pill. Sexual union most fully manifests its splendor and the "language of the body" speaks loudest when a child is conceived. By its very nature as an image of the Trinity, marriage is supposed to be a family affair.

JOHN PAUL II
In His Own Words

One can speak of moral good and evil according to whether this relationship makes such a "unity of the body" true and whether or not *it gives to that unity the character of a truthful sign.*

(TOB 37:6)

According to the criterion of this truth, which must be expressed in the "language of the body," the conjugal act "means" not only love, but also potential fruitfulness, and therefore it cannot be deprived of its full and adequate meaning by means of artificial interventions. In the conjugal act, it is not licit to separate artificially the unitive meaning from the procreative meaning, because the one as well as the other belong to the innermost truth of the conjugal act. The one is realized together with the other and, in a certain way, the one through the other.

(TOB 123:6)

THINGS TO PONDER AND SHARE

1. Describe a time in your life when your actions "spoke louder than your words."

2. Why is "truth-telling" such an important part of human language and human existence?

3. How is sex "significant"? Why is this message so important in a time when sex is treated very casually?

4. When those who aren't married engage in sexual relations, they *do not* "tell the truth" with their bodies. Why? How does this relate to the sixth commandment, "You shall not commit adultery"?

5. Why is sex exclusively for husband and wife, and exclusively for a man and a woman? Why must sex be a sincere giving that is open to life? What acts communicate these truths and what acts contradict them?

6. Do you agree that lusting has become part of the cultural fabric? What are some examples of this? Have you recognized the pervasiveness of the problem of Internet pornography? Share your perspective on this problem.

7. How did you feel when you read that in God's plan sex is supposed to be a source of joy and enjoyment for the spouses, and that sexual feelings and sexual pleasure are *very good*? Were you surprised that this is

what the Church teaches? Why or why not? Can you explain why the pursuit of sexual pleasure outside of the gift of one's whole self in marriage distorts God's plan?

··READ THE CATECHISM OF THE CATHOLIC CHURCH ····

nos. 1640, 2332, 2336, 2350–2363

CHAPTER 15

A FAMILY AFFAIR

Blessed is every one who fears the LORD,
*   who walks in his ways!*
You shall eat the fruit of the labor of your hands;
*   you shall be happy, and it shall be well with you.*
Your wife will be like a fruitful vine
*   within your house;*
your children will be like olive shoots
*   around your table. . . .*

Lo, sons are a heritage from the LORD,
*   the fruit of the womb a reward.*
Like arrows in the hand of a warrior
*   are the sons of one's youth.*
Happy is the man who has
*   his quiver full of them!*

—Psalm 128:1–3, 127:3–5a

THE ROLE OF THE CHRISTIAN FAMILY IN THE WORLD

My favorite baseball team of all time is the 1979 Pittsburgh Pirates. Though we lived in New Jersey, my dad was born and raised in Pittsburgh, and that meant that I really had no say in the matter—somehow genetically I was both a Pirates and a Steelers fan. Being the devoted son of a Steel-town native, I passionately rooted for these teams during every game. I had my Steelers "terrible towel" in my hand in the winter and wore my "Bucs" square-top baseball cap on my head all summer.

Then came the year to rival all years: 1979. That year the Steelers had defeated the Dallas Cowboys in Super Bowl XIII by a three-point margin, and our beloved Pirates slugged their way to the World Series. They faced the Baltimore Orioles and, to tell you the truth, the first half of that series cast a pall over the Hajduk house. The Pirates were down 3–1, and no team in Major League history had ever come back from that kind of a deficit. As much as we might have doubted, however, we never lost hope. And it was all because of the Pirates' motto during that season: "We Are Family."

I can still see Willie Stargell (arguably one of the best homerun hitters ever and the veteran of the squad affectionately known as "Pops") pulling the team together. I can still hear that song by Sister Sledge: "We are family . . ." The fans got up and sang at good ol' Pops' bidding. Everybody was united. Everybody believed. Everybody supported and encouraged each other—fans and players alike. We followed Pops' lead—and it wound up making baseball history, as the Pirates rallied to win three straight! As silly as it sounds, I cried that day. I think my father did too.

Remember how I said that by its very nature as an image of the Trinity marriage is supposed to be a family affair? This is also true of its nature as an image of Jesus' marriage with the Church—a union that created the ever growing "family of God" through the "birthing waters" of Baptism. Marriage and sex are not just about a "you" and a "me"—they're about a "we." For this reason, sexual union always includes and never intentionally excludes the child. In a sense, in each and every sexual union the man and woman recognize and rediscover the profound meaning of their masculinity and femininity. By joining together in such an intimate way as to become "one flesh," they open themselves up to the fullest realization of that "one flesh" union: the conception of a child. That is, they open themselves up to the *possibility* of fatherhood and motherhood. Fundamentally, they say with their bodies as well as their souls, "We are family. We will—if God wills—no longer to be two, but three." This is all part of what spouses communicate in the "body language" of sexual union.

THE MISSION OF THE MARRIED

"Be fruitful and multiply" (Gen 1:28) was the original blessing of the Creator not only on the first married couple, but also on every married couple that would be modeled upon them. In God's plan, the heavenly Father calls spouses to cooperate with him in the task of enlarging and enriching *his own family*. Through their openness to life, spouses actually participate in the awesome mission of creating new persons made in God's image and likeness. Thus, the fundamental task of the family is to serve and foster life: both natural life and eternal life. This is why the procreation and education of children are not something "added onto" marriage, but rather are at the very heart of marriage itself.

CHECK IT OUT

For more about God's plan for spouses to cooperate with him in giving life, read Pope John Paul II, *The Role of the Christian Family in the Modern World*, no. 28.

Since the family has this fundamental task to serve and foster both natural and eternal life, it has the responsibility to proclaim and share the Gospel, to teach and learn love, and to provide for the needs of earthly life. The family, sometimes called the domestic Church, can, in a very real and true way, claim for itself the titles and the mission assigned to the Church. The family is a "sacrament of salvation" that "makes Christ present" in the world. As such, it is called to proclaim the Gospel in word and deed, teach obedience to God's commandments, witness to the sanctity of life, set an example of love, and serve the poor and vulnerable. The Christian family indeed has a mission and a ministry—first to its members, since "charity begins at home," but then to the Church and to the world.

Parents have the inalienable right and irreplaceable duty to educate their children and form them in the faith. They are the first and most important teachers that their children will ever have. They are responsible not only for the physical well-being of their children—food, clothing, shelter, education, health care, and the like—but also for the spiritual well-being of their children. That means that Christian parents must, to the best of their ability, ensure that their children come to know, love, and serve the Lord Jesus and his Church. Their primary task is to form saints, not necessarily scholars; to help their children get to heaven, not necessarily Harvard. That's not to say that parents shouldn't be concerned with their children's educational future or that they should somehow be disappointed if their children go to a top tier school. Neither does it mean they should undervalue the material needs of the body. But it does mean that parents need to put "first things first." Life is short. Eternity is . . . well . . . eternal. And all temporal goods find their true value only in light of their ultimate purpose: to equip us to love as God loves and give the sincere gift of ourselves in and through our bodies; to empower us, through our unique and individual giftedness, to be an unrepeatable physical image of God in the world.

Therefore, this total formation as a human being, body and soul, is really meant to enable children to become *the gifts that they are*: gifts for the Church *and* for the world. Parents are called to raise their children to become productive members of society who will offer their gifts, indeed *offer themselves*, to help transform what Saint John Paul II called the "culture of death"

into a "culture of life and love" by promoting all that is good, true, and beautiful. In so doing, the family clearly shares in the life and mission of the Church and participates in the development of society, which are two more of its tasks (see Saint John Paul II, *The Role of the Christian Family in the Modern World*, no. 17). The family is the school of love, where children learn to give the sincere gift of themselves in and through their bodies. The family is the domestic Church in which parents nourish their children with the word of God and teach them all that Jesus commanded, so they can become co-workers with the Holy Spirit in building up God's kingdom and in renewing the face of the earth!

> **Did U Know**
>
> Parents are called to give the sincere gift of themselves in and through their bodies for the good of their children. In this way they learn daily what it means to love as Jesus loves. Since loving as God loves is the way to be fully human and happy, this is how children contribute to the good of their parents. In fact, children help parents live a rich life and get to heaven!

RESPONSIBLE PARENTHOOD

Now, you may wonder: If the fundamental task of the family is to serve and foster life, are there ever times when having another child might actually *not* serve and foster life? The short answer is "yes." That's why the Church speaks about "responsible parenthood." However, we need to properly understand exactly what that means.

"Responsible parenthood" means that spouses are called to intelligently and willingly cooperate with God in the procreation of children. They are not called to merely submit themselves to biological processes, but rather to act, in a certain sense, as "interpreters" of God's plan by carefully considering their genuine good and that of their family.

This is why the Church has never proposed that a couple should have as many children as physically possible. While children are always a blessing and never a burden, having more children than one can reasonably

> **FOR YOUR CONSIDERATION**
>
> In *The Joy of Love*, no. 222, Pope Francis writes beautifully about this process of discernment.

provide for may be considered *irresponsible* and may demonstrate a lack of consideration for the overall good of the family. Christian spouses may have serious and just reasons for deciding to refrain from conceiving another child for the time being.

Notice that I said "serious and just" reasons and "for the time being." Unless a couple has serious and just reasons to avoid having children, they shouldn't do anything to avoid having them. Rather, they should welcome children with "the generosity appropriate to responsible parenthood." However, if a couple has "serious and just" reasons, they may find it necessary to avoid conceiving a child until these reasons no longer exist. Clearly, such reasons could exist for quite a long time, even indefinitely. But the couple should take the view that this time of avoiding the conception of a child is temporary and not permanent, that they are *postponing* children and not *excluding* them.

SERIOUS AND JUST REASONS VS. THE CONTRACEPTIVE MENTALITY

It is important to note that these serious and just reasons have little to do with lifestyle or social status. They have to do with *hardship*. If such reasons were about lifestyle or social status, they wouldn't be serious or just at all, but would merely be a disguise for materialism or for what Saint John Paul II called a "contraceptive mentality."

A contraceptive mentality does not approach the conception of children with openness and generosity. It tends to pit human life itself against a variety of personal goals: career, class, financial independence, material possessions, and the like. Those who think in this way select the number of children they will have (if they decide to have any at all) according to the lifestyle they wish to maintain. A contraceptive mentality suffers from inverted thinking and betrays, whether consciously or not, an *anti-life* attitude that treats persons as objects rather than gifts and views procreation as an obstacle to personal fulfillment. It is easy to see how abortion becomes an extension of the contraceptive mentality and is then seen as the "only possible decisive response to failed contraception."[13] And nothing contradicts God's original plan for human love, human sexuality, marriage, and family life more than abortion. Now, it is often said that women who have abortions typically aren't having them because of "freedom of choice" but because they feel like they have *no choice*. So, it is important to look upon them in compassion and non-judgment, acknowledging that we do not know the state of their hearts and the many factors that influenced them to make such a tragic, and often

"I would now like to say a special word to women who have had an abortion. The Church is aware of the many factors which may have influenced your decision, and she does not doubt that in many cases it was a painful and even shattering decision. The wound in your heart may not yet have healed. Certainly what happened was and remains terribly wrong. But do not give in to discouragement and do not lose hope. Try rather to understand what happened and face it honestly. If you have not already done so, give yourselves over with humility and trust to repentance. The Father of mercies is ready to give you his forgiveness and his peace in the sacrament of Reconciliation. To the same Father and his mercy you can with sure hope entrust your child. With the friendly and expert help and advice of other people, and as a result of your own painful experience, you can be among the most eloquent defenders of everyone's right to life. Through your commitment to life, whether by accepting the birth of other children or by welcoming and caring for those most in need of someone to be close to them, you will become promoters of a new way of looking at human life."

—Saint John Paul II,
The Gospel of Life, no. 99

times "painful and shattering," decision (see Saint John Paul II, *The Gospel of Life*, no. 99). Yet, whatever the reasons people use to try to justify it, abortion involves the denial of God as the sovereign Lord of life, the refusal to love as God loves and to give the sincere gift of oneself to another person "that they might have life and have it abundantly" (Jn 10:10), and an attack on the greatest gift and blessing of all: the child, who is unique and irreplaceable.

> Many women who have had abortions suffer terribly, but all too often alone and in silence. People are frequently unaware of the compassionate programs that seek to help women find hope and healing after abortion. One such program is Project Rachel (www.hopeafterabortion.com). Do you know someone who has been wounded by an abortion decision? Please share this information with them.

A married couple also shouldn't postpone conceiving children out of a misguided, albeit understandable, desire to give their children everything—whether it be the best clothes, the best "toys," or even providing full tuition for the best college. I've never met a person who came from a large family who didn't love it or who would have "traded" their brothers and sisters for more stuff or their own room.

All this being said, let me share some examples of what might be serious and just reasons to postpone pregnancy. Some cases involve emotional or physical sickness or hardship. In other situations, parents justly desire to space their children for the emotional and physical well-being of the mother. A family could be facing financial difficulties that make it practically impossible to reasonably provide for the basic needs (food, clothing, shelter, etc.) of the children they already have. Sometimes an already living child is very ill or has a disability that requires much time, attention, and resources. Some marriages become unstable, especially where there is spousal abuse, lack of spousal support, or domestic violence. These are just some examples of serious and just reasons.[14]

Unfortunately, not all situations are equally easy to determine. That's why the Church teaches that, ultimately, the couple themselves must decide whether they have serious and just reasons to postpone pregnancy. The couple makes this prudential judgment in prayer, mindful of the moral principles the Church proposes, and with a careful examination of their motives.[15] The Church recommends seeking the advice of friends and family, as well as that of a spiritual director (like a priest, religious brother or sister, or a lay professional) before reaching a conclusion. At the same time, the Church also encourages families to trust in the Lord to provide for their needs, even in the midst of hardship.

NATURAL FAMILY PLANNING

What if a couple determines that they have serious and just reasons to avoid conceiving a child for the time being? If the sincere gift of the spouses' whole selves to one another in sexual union must always be open to the gift of the child, does that mean that that couple must abstain from sex until those serious reasons cease to exist? The answer is yes and no.

Admittedly, this may not seem like much of an answer. While sexual union must remain open to life, we know that a child is not conceived in every sexual union. God wills this and has created the woman's body this way. As the sovereign Lord of life, God ultimately determines which marital acts will result in the conception of a child. And spouses commit no evil by their mutual decision to refrain from sexual activity.

Based on these facts, spouses can use Natural Family Planning (NFP) to avoid conceiving a child for serious and just reasons while remaining open to life.

A woman's fertility cycle, which recurs about every twenty-eight days, can be divided into "phases." God has designed a woman's body in such a way that conception is possible during only one of these phases. Basically, NFP helps the spouses detect when the woman has entered or has left her "fertile phase" by observing certain changes in her body. Spouses who wish to postpone pregnancy would reserve all sexual relations for the infertile phases of the woman's cycle. This would be consistent with what was discussed above, because the spouses do not do anything directly to *make* their sexual unions infertile—they just *are infertile*, and naturally so. This would be similar to spouses having sex who know that they are perpetually infertile (sterile), or when a woman is either in her post-child-bearing years or already pregnant. The Church has never said that it would be wrong for such people to have sex. Why? Because they haven't done anything *to make* their sexual acts infertile, even if they know they will be. The Church has also never said that the intention to avoid having children for a time due to serious and just reasons is a bad intention. In fact, it's a good one! Rather, the Church has said that the way in which spouses accomplish this must authentically express God's love and the sincere gift of their whole selves, which they promised in their marriage vows, for they must always "tell the truth" with their bodies.

Because spouses who utilize NFP have neither done anything to *make* their sexual unions infertile nor to directly eliminate the possibility of conception, they remain "open to life" and a sign of the communion of persons within the Trinity and the love of Christ for the Church. This is what makes NFP very different from contraception. The way a couple actually avoids conception with NFP is by choosing not to give the gift of themselves to one another in a sexual way during a certain time in the woman's monthly cycle. When they do choose to give this gift, they do nothing to prevent the conception of a child if God wills it. That is, they say

Did U Know

For just reasons, spouses may wish to space the births of their children. It is their duty to make certain that their desire is not motivated by selfishness but is in conformity with the generosity appropriate to responsible parenthood (see *CCC*, no. 2368).

"yes" to the child that might be conceived during that union. With contraception, a couple directly and intentionally causes their sexual union to be infertile and seeks to eliminate the possibility of procreation. They, in effect, say "no" to the child that might be conceived during that union.

But NFP isn't only about postponing pregnancy. NFP can help spouses who are having difficulty conceiving a child. By using NFP they can identify the woman's fertile phase and thereby significantly increase the chances of becoming pregnant. NFP is also instrumental in scientific advances, such as NaProTECHNOLOGY (Natural Procreative Technology) developed by the Pope Paul VI Institute in Nebraska. This method helps couples to evaluate and treat a variety of women's health issues and conceive children when such conception was previously thought impossible. This leads to a very sensitive subject: infertility.

INFERTILITY AND THE CALL TO FRUITFULNESS IN MARRIAGE

My wife and I have never had difficulty conceiving children. Thus, we can never fully understand the pain that infertile couples experience. However, I have met many people who have had such difficulty, even within my own family. You might also know someone who struggles with this. I have seen the sorrow that comes from having an incredible desire to have children, yet not being able to. It is very heartbreaking to watch; I can only imagine what it's like to live through.

Let me repeat that a *naturally* infertile couple, who through no deliberate choice is physically unable to bear children, does not have "less" of a marriage than a couple who has been blessed with many children. This couple is certainly not "cursed" or "judged" by God as not deserving of children. In fact, as an image of the Trinity, their marriage is still called to "give life" and be fruitful, though for them this takes on another form. That's why the Church encourages such couples to adopt children or to offer themselves more fully to other work that "fosters life," such as "various forms of education-al work, and assistance to other families and to poor or handicapped children" (Saint John Paul II, *The Role of the Christian Family in the Modern World*, no. 14).

This being said, in God's plan sexual union and children go together and cannot be deliber-ately separated from one another. This applies not only to preventing preg-nancy, but also to "achieving" pregnancy. Contraception and the like *separate babies from sex*; in vitro fertil-ization, artificial insemination, and other replacement reproductive procedures *separate sex from babies*. Every child has the right to be the fruit of the total self-giving

> **FOR YOUR CONSIDERATION**
>
> "A child deserves to be born of that love, and not by any other means, for 'he or she is not something owed to one, but is a gift,' which is 'the fruit of the specific act of the conjugal love of the parents.'"
>
> —Pope Francis, *The Joy of Love*, no. 81

of his or her parents. Each has the right to be conceived in love as the fruit of the one flesh union of their mother and father. Children are meant by God to be "begotten, not made." They are meant to be received from him as a gift.

The desire and instinct for children is powerful. Few people wouldn't sympathize with an infertile couple that seeks their own biological children, and it is very understandable why so many turn to reproductive technologies as the solution. We shouldn't judge these couples. Yet, such technologies objectively change the creation of a child from an act of *procreation* into an act of mere *reproduction*. In *procreation*, the couple acknowledges God as the Lord of life. In *reproduction*, parents and doctors *assume the role* of the Lord of life, try to "replace the Creator" (*The Joy of Love*, no. 56), and treat the child as if he or she is a product to be manufactured.

Did U Know

Did you know that it is possible for a person conceived through *in vitro* to have five parents? These include sperm and egg donors, the man and woman who are having the procedure done, and a surrogate mother to carry the child in her womb and give birth. It could be even more than five if the couple who had the procedure done (who would be the ones called the mother and father) get divorced and remarried. Divorced couples have already fought court cases over custody of frozen embryos. These are a few more reasons why these technologies can be so problematic.

Besides this, many of the human beings made by in vitro fertilization are either killed or cryogenically frozen (for the couple to use in the future). The number of human beings "on ice" in laboratories all over the world is too high to count. Once the couple has had the number of children they desire, they usually either have their children destroyed or donated for research. These are just a few examples of how these technologies treat people as products—to be disposed of if they are no longer "useful."

However, I want to stress that *how* a person is conceived does not make him or her any more or less of a person. A person is a person *no matter how they were created*. It would be downright ridiculous to say that a child conceived through in vitro fertilization or artificial insemination (or even through fornication, adultery, or rape for that matter) are somehow less human or less valuable than anyone else. God is the Lord and Giver of life! All human beings are created by him in his image and have an eternal destiny. All human life is precious. All human life is sacred. All human life, no matter the circumstances in which it is created, ought to be celebrated. This is a given. But precisely because human life is so valuable, how it is created takes on great importance.

In this chapter we have seen how God's plan for humanity is a "family plan." In fact, by his saving death and resurrection and his gift of the Spirit, Jesus has called all human beings to become part of God's family, the Church. And just as fathers and mothers are called to serve a natural family, priests and those in the consecrated life are called to serve God's family.

JOHN PAUL II
In His Own Words

The first parents transmit to all human parents . . . the fundamental truth about the birth of man in the image of God, according to the laws of nature. In this new man . . . the same "image of God" is reproduced every time, the image of that God who constituted the humanity of the first man, "God created man in his image . . . ; male and female he created them" (Gen 1:27).

(TOB 21:6)

The words of Genesis that bear witness to the first birth of man on earth contain, at the same time, everything that one can and should say about the dignity of human generation.

(TOB 21:7)

THINGS TO PONDER AND SHARE

1. Spouses have a mission to co-operate with God in enlarging and enriching his own family. If couples understood this mission better, how would it affect their view of the procreation and education of children?

2. What ought to be the primary concern of parents regarding their children? Why?

3. What is a "contraceptive mentality"? How is it expressed today? How is abortion an extension of it?

4. When a couple has serious and just reasons to postpone conceiving a child, why does using NFP respect God's plan, but using contraception does not?

5. Why are reproductive technologies, such as in vitro fertilization and artificial insemination, morally problematic?

6. Why is adoption and serving others such a rich part of our Church's teachings on the family?

7. Do you know any families that are truly "communities of life and love"? Describe the qualities that make them so.

·· READ THE CATECHISM OF THE CATHOLIC CHURCH ·····

nos. 1655–1657, 2270–2275, 2366–2379

CHAPTER 16

THE FINAL CHAPTER

Then I heard what seemed to be the voice of a great multitude, like the sound of many waters and like the sound of mighty thunderpeals, crying, "Hallelujah! For the Lord our God the Almighty reigns. Let us rejoice and exult and give him the glory, for the marriage of the Lamb has come, and his Bride has made herself ready; it was granted her to be clothed with fine linen, bright and pure"—for the fine linen is the righteous deeds of the saints. And the angel said to me, "Write this: Blessed are those who are invited to the marriage supper of the Lamb."

—Revelation 19:6–9

THE HEAVENLY MARRIAGE AND THE CELIBATE LIFE

In his popular book, *The 7 Habits of Highly Effective People*, Stephen Covey suggests that if a person is to be truly effective, whether in business or in life, then he or she must always "begin with the end in mind." Covey even goes so far as to ask his readers to imagine what they would want different people to say about them at their funeral. Exercises like this, he believes, can help us to pinpoint the sort of persons we should be each and every day. The Scriptures challenge us to do the same: "In all you do, remember the end of your life, and then you will never sin" (Sir 7:36).

Well, what is the "end" that we should keep in mind? It's our eternal destiny, of course! It's the meeting that each of us has with God at the "hour of our death." You see, the point of going back to "the beginning" isn't *only* so we can make ourselves ready to enter into an earthly marriage and enjoy earthly happiness. It's so we can make ourselves ready to enter into the *ultimate marriage* with God in heaven and enjoy eternal happiness! You could almost say that the real point of *The Cosmic Prequel* is to prepare for and get to *The Final Chapter*: our marriage with God!

Now, I know the whole idea of "marrying" God may sound a bit bizarre, but it's really not if you think about it. Didn't God teach Adam in his "loneliness" that besides him there is "no other" and that every other "communion of persons" is secondary to the one with him? Didn't Jesus teach us that the first and greatest commandment is to love God with our whole heart, mind, soul, and strength (body), and then "our neighbor as ourselves"? Didn't Saint Paul tell us that we "are not our own," that we belong to God and are called to become "one body" with him and "bear fruit"? I don't know about you, but this sounds an awful lot like marriage to me!

MARRIAGE IN HEAVEN?

So does that mean there is marriage in heaven as there is on earth? I think it's a perfectly natural thing for people to wonder about. The question itself reveals just how important marriage and sex are to us and how much happiness they bring when they are lived the way God intended. They are so important to us that we hope they last forever. They bring us so much happiness that we almost cannot conceive of heaven being without them and still being worthy of the name.

However, when seen in light of our ultimate "marriage" with God, it becomes clear that the answer is "no"—at least not in the way marriage exists on earth. When Jesus was asked the question: "Is there marriage in heaven as there is on earth?" he said that "in the resurrection they neither marry nor are given in marriage" (Mt 22:30). At first, this may seem odd, or even harsh to us, especially considering that Jesus thought so highly of marriage that he took us back to "the beginning" to discover God's original plan for it. And yet, if you really think about God's original plan for life, love, marriage, and sex, it makes perfect sense.

Jesus said there's no marriage in heaven because he knew that *earthly marriage simply "pointed to" the marriage of God and his people.* Earthly marriage is only a "sign" and a foretaste of what's in store for us when we enter the pearly gates. In fact, Jesus used the image of a wedding feast to describe heaven (see Mt 25:1–13). And in the Scriptures, Jesus and his Father are identified as the Bridegroom (see Is 54:5, 62:5; Mt 9:15; Jn 3:29), and Israel, the Church, *and ourselves* as the Bride (see Is 54:6; Jer 2:2; Song 4:8–12; Eph 5:22–23; Rev 19:7). So Jesus gave this answer to teach us that the "marriage" between God and us was the whole point of earthly marriage from "the beginning."

Yet, Jesus never excludes the possibility of having a unique relationship with your earthly spouse in heaven either, and this makes sense. I mean, we will still know our parents as parents, our siblings as siblings, and our friends as friends, won't we? Don't people find comfort in the belief that they will see their deceased loved ones again, perhaps even a child lost to miscarriage? Actually, when we become fully one with God, we will also become fully one with all these people too. These relationships do not disappear or lose their unique character in heaven; rather these relationships are perfected. And that means that the relationship between spouses will be everything it was on earth but made perfect!

However, since there isn't marriage in heaven in the earthly sense, you may be wondering, "Is there sex in heaven?" Well, that all depends on what you mean by "sex." If by sex you mean "gender," there obviously *is* sex in heaven. In heaven we will be either male or female. This will be true *before* the resurrection of the dead, when our soul separates from our body and dwells with God, because our masculinity or femininity is not merely a biological reality, but also a spiritual one. It will certainly be true *after* our resurrection, when we are reunited with our bodies with all their masculine and feminine parts and become the body-persons God intended us to be from "the beginning."

And since we will be body-persons for all eternity, eternity will be a "body-soul" experience! Heaven will not just be about a feeling of peace and fulfillment in our soul, but it will also be about the most radical bodily pleasure ever imagined! We will experience heaven with *our senses and our souls*. As I said earlier in the book, though we do not know exactly what heaven will be like, I firmly believe that in heaven we will "rediscover" all the good things we experienced in our earthly lives, like sunsets, mountain ranges, music, and food. Yet, they will all be clearly seen for what they are: expressions of God's sincere gift of himself to us and of him pouring himself out for us and lavishing his love on us (TOB 65:5, 68:4). And they will be so dramatically better than their earthly counterparts that they will appear entirely new to us. In God, not only will we find our earthly relationships perfected, but we will find all that is good, true, and beautiful on earth perfected as well!

Although there will be sex in heaven in the sense of masculinity and femininity, and there will be the most radical bodily pleasure ever imagined, there *will not* be any sex in heaven in the sense of *sexual activity*. And simply put, this is because there *isn't* marriage in heaven in the way there is on earth. Earthly marriage and sexual union are a package deal.

When you think about it, the whole purpose of earthly marriage and sexual union will be rendered obsolete by our "marriage" with God in heaven. Sexual communion is a mere shadow of the communion with God for which we were all created. The "end of time" will mean the end of procreation as we know it, since body-persons are not created *in* heaven, but are created on earth *for* heaven. And the bliss of our union with God will make even the most pleasurable sexual experience on earth seem like nothing in comparison.

Additionally, on earth the union of the spouses' bodies in sexual union is supposed to bring about a true communion of persons. *The goal of bodily union was always personal union.* As we already mentioned, in heaven the personal union between the spouses is made perfect. They will be closer than they ever have been or could be before; they will be *more one* than they were in sexual union!

CELIBACY: THE HEAVENLY MARRIAGE IN ADVANCE

This discussion about our heavenly "marriage with God" sheds new light on the *celibate life*. Celibacy is often viewed as a cross that a man or woman must bear if they are to become a priest or religious brother or sister. If someone views it that way, then he or she *should not* become a priest or a religious brother or sister. The celibate life, properly understood, does not reject marriage at all—instead it trades earthly marriage for the heavenly marriage "in advance"! Celibacy is about giving the sincere gift of one's whole self to God—*the Bridegroom*—alone. It is about dedicating oneself completely to the Church—*the family of God*—and to building a culture of life and love. It is about making *vows to God* similar to the way spouses make vows to each other. Therefore, celibacy is, to a certain extent, a "living out" of the heavenly state while still on earth! The value of celibacy does not come from someone "giving up" marriage and sex; it comes from someone "giving themselves" totally to God for the sake of the kingdom of God. And, by the way, a *single person* could in fact be called to a life of celibacy as part of giving themselves totally to God and the Church *without* being called to the priesthood or consecrated life. Such a person may make a private promise of chastity to God. (This is not the same as someone finding themselves single, though they would really like to be married, and following God's plan by abstaining from sex.)

Notable Quotable

The free choice of sacred celibacy. . . signifies a love without reservations; it stimulates to a charity which is open to all.

—Blessed Paul VI

Through a commitment to a life of prayer, a celibate man or woman devotes him- or herself to seeking the presence of God and forming a communion of persons with him on *this side of eternity*. And through a commitment to a life of service, a celibate man or woman devotes him- or herself to loving as God loves in the most extremely inclusive way!

It must be admitted that, while the love of a husband and wife is called to be inclusive by accepting children lovingly from the Lord, spouses are rightly preoccupied with and focused on the good of each other and their children. In this sense, their "inclusiveness" is tempered by their state in life. As Saint Paul said, "the married man is anxious about worldly affairs, how to please his wife . . . the married woman is anxious about worldly affairs, how to please her husband" (1 Cor 7:33–34). In special instances, the call to a particular ministry or public service may be so strong that a family chooses to make great sacrifices for the sake of it (I think of someone like Reverend Martin Luther King, Jr., for example). But this is an exceptional and heroic choice. Even in such a case, the husband and wife cannot neglect the genuine needs of one another or their children, for this is their *vocation*. Married couples actually live out their baptismal call to love as God loves in and through their bodies by being a husband-father or wife-mother. Therefore, they need to be true to their state in life and the limits placed on it. Saint Paul demanded this when he said, "Every one should remain in the state in which he was called" (1 Cor 7:20).

On the other hand, the love of a celibate man or woman is free from these constraints and therefore able to be more inclusive and universal in its scope. As Saint Paul said, "The unmarried man is anxious about the affairs of the Lord . . . the unmarried woman or girl is anxious about the affairs of the Lord, how to be holy in body and spirit" (1 Cor 7:32, 34). Due to their state in life, celibate men and women are more available to serve God's people with abandon. Their sincere gift of their whole selves "gives life" to others, though in a different way from most married couples. For example, a priest gives supernatural life to others through Baptism, and a religious brother or sister gives life to others by, let's say, working with the poor or teaching the young.

Those who enter the priesthood or consecrated life do not "check in" their masculinity or femininity at the door of the cathedral. They still have masculine and feminine gifts and corresponding masculine and feminine ways of serving. You may not have ever thought about it, but we call them father, mother, sister, and brother for a good reason. They serve the family of God, the Church, in a way similar to the way a father, mother, "older" sister, or "older" brother serves their biological family.

It should also be noted that the family, in turn, serves the priesthood and the consecrated life. The family is the rich soil in which religious vocations grow, for in the family a person is formed in the faith, develops a love of prayer, and learns how to love as God loves by serving his or her parents and siblings.

So, *The Final Chapter* makes it clear that *marriage is for everyone* and that *marriage is the meaning of life*! God's original plan for life, love, marriage, and sex is the key to happiness—whether you are single, married, a priest, or a consecrated person. Jesus reminds us of *The Cosmic Prequel*, bringing us back to "the beginning," so we can love as he loves in and through our bodies and fulfill the purpose of our existence. Treasure this truth; hold it close to your heart. I promise you that you will know a joy you never dreamed possible. You will make yourself ready, not only for earthly marriage, but also for the heavenly marriage to which you were called before the foundation of the world.

And I hope to see you there!

JOHN PAUL II
In His Own Words

When Christ speaks about the resurrection, he shows at the same time that even the human body will participate, in its own way, in this eschatological [ultimate] experience of truth and love, united with the vision of God "face to face."

(TOB 67:4)

[The] human being (male and female) who—in the earthly situation, in which "they take wife and take husband" (Lk 20:34)—of his own free will chooses [celibacy] "for the kingdom of heaven" shows that in this reign, that is, the "other world" of the resurrection, "they will take neither wife nor husband" (Mk 12:25), because God will be "all in all" (1 Cor 15:28).

(TOB 75:1)

THINGS TO PONDER AND SHARE

1. Name a time when "beginning with the end in mind" made you more effective and successful.

2. How does *The Cosmic Prequel* help us to prepare for and get to *The Final Chapter*?

3. How *is* there and *isn't* there marriage in heaven?

4. How *is* there and *isn't* there sex in heaven?

5. What do you imagine heaven will be like?

6. How does the celibate life anticipate the heavenly marriage rather than reject marriage as some think it does?

··READ THE CATECHISM OF THE CATHOLIC CHURCH ····

nos. 997–1001, 1023–1029, 1042–1050, 1060, 1612, 1618–1620, 2348–2349

NOTES

1. My faith story: http://lifeteen.com/blog/jp2-rescue-healing-treehugger-theology. My nun story: http://lifeteen.com/blog/really-like-married-jesus/.

2. This is found in his work, *The Great Divorce*.

3. See William May, *An Introduction to Moral Theology* (Huntington, IN: Our Sunday Visitor, 1994), 23–24.

4. These words are attributed to Samuel Smiles.

5. This is found in a famous work titled *Mere Christianity*.

6. Karol Wojtyla (Pope John Paul II), *Love and Responsibility* (Boston: Pauline Books & Media, 2013), 26.

7. Saint John Damascene, *De fide orth.* 3, 24: *PG* 94,1089C, as cited in the *CCC*, no. 2559.

8. A paraphrase of Saint Teresa of Avila, *The Book of Her Life*, 8, 5, in *The Collected Works of St. Teresa of Avila*, trans. K. Kavanaugh, OCD, and O. Rodriguez, OCD (Washington, DC: Institute of Carmelite Studies, 1976), I, 67, as cited in *CCC*, no. 2709.

9. Thomas Aquinas, *Summa Theologiae*, part 3, ques. 73, art. 3, ad. 3.

10. http://www.nsvrc.org/sites/default/files/publications_ nsvrc_factsheet_media-packet_statistics-about-sexual- violence_0.pdf.

11. For more technical details on this, see: http://www. lifeissues.org/2014/09/abortifacients-overview/.

12. For details, see: http://www.nrlc.org/uploads/fact sheets/FS01AbortionintheUS.pdf.

13. John Paul II, *The Gospel of Life*, no. 13.

14. See Paul VI, *Of Human Life*, no. 10. See also, "How should a couple discern 'just' and 'serious' reasons for post-poning pregnancy?" from Jason Adams, *Called to Give Life* (Dayton, OH: One More Soul, 2003), 123–128.

15. See Vatican II, *Pastoral Constitution on the Church in the Modern World*, no. 50.

BIBLIOGRAPHY

Adams, Jason. *Called to Give Life*. Dayton, OH: One More Soul, 2003.

Aristotle. *Basic Works of Aristotle*. Edited Richard McKeon. New York: Random House, Inc., 1941.

Benedict XVI. *God Is Love*. Boston: Pauline Books & Media, 2006.

Cantalamessa, Raniero. *Jesus Christ, the Holy One of God*. Collegeville, MN: The Liturgical Press, 1991.

Catechism of the Catholic Church. Libreria Editrice Vaticana, 1994.

Francis. *The Joy of Love*. Boston: Pauline Books & Media, 2016.

Hogan, Rev. Richard, and Rev. John LeVoir. *Covenant of Love: Pope John Paul II on Sexuality, Marriage, and Family in the Modern World*. San Francisco: Ignatius Press, 1985.

John XXIII. *Christianity and Social Progress*. Vatican online translation, 1961.

John Paul II. *The Church: Mystery, Sacrament, Community*. Boston: Pauline Books & Media, 1998.

———. *The Gospel of Life*. Boston: Pauline Books & Media, 1995.

———. *Man and Woman He Created Them: A Theology of the Body*. Translated by Michael Waldstein. Boston: Pauline Books & Media, 2006.

———. *The Role of the Christian Family in the Modern World*. Boston: Pauline Books & Media, 1981.

May, William. *An Introduction to Moral Theology*. Huntington, IN: Our Sunday Visitor, 1994.

Paul VI. *Of Human Life*. Boston: Pauline Books & Media, 1968. Second Vatican Council. Dogmatic Constitution on the Church. Vatican online translation, 1964.

———. *Dogmatic Constitution on Divine Revelation*. Vatican online translation, 1965.

———. *Pastoral Constitution on the Church in the Modern World*. Vatican online translation, 1965.

West, Christopher. *Good News about Sex & Marriage: Answers to Your Honest Questions About Catholic Teaching*. Ann Arbor, MI: Servant Publications, 2000.

———. *Theology of the Body Explained: A Commentary of John Paul II's Man and Woman He Created Them*. Boston: Pauline Books & Media, 2007.

Wojtyla, Karol. *Love and Responsibility*. Translated by Grzegorz Ignatik. Boston: Pauline Books & Media, 2013.

Zuck, Roy, B. *The Speaker's Quote Book*. Grand Rapids, MI: Kregel Publications, 1997.

David Hajduk, Ph.D. has over twenty-five years of experience in religious education and youth, family life, and pro-life ministries. Since 1998, he has been a member of the Religious Studies Department at Delbarton School in Morristown, New Jersey, and since 2002 has been the Director of Campus Ministry. He is also an Adjunct Professor of Systematic Theology at Immaculate Conception Seminary School of Theology at Seton Hall University. David is widely respected as a dynamic speaker and teacher. He received his doctorate in theology from Maryvale Institute in Birmingham, UK, and wrote his dissertation on the thought of Saint John Paul II. A husband and a father, David resides in New Jersey with his wife, Shannon, and their children.

Go to David's website to read his spiritual reflections or to reach out to him by email: www.thelifeofthebeloved.com.

BOOKS & MEDIA

A mission of the Daughters of St. Paul

As apostles of Jesus Christ, evangelizing today's world:

We are CALLED to holiness

by God's living Word and Eucharist.

We COMMUNICATE the Gospel message

through our lives and through all

available forms of media.

We SERVE the Church

by responding to the hopes and needs

of all people with the Word of God,

in the spirit of St. Paul.

For more information visit our website: www.pauline.org.

BOOKS & MEDIA

The Daughters of St. Paul operate book and media centers at the following addresses. Visit, call, or write the one nearest you today, or find us at www.paulinestore.org.

CALIFORNIA

3908 Sepulveda Blvd, Culver City, CA 90230 — 310-397-8676

3250 Middlefield Road, Menlo Park, CA 94025 — 650-369-4230

FLORIDA

145 S.W. 107th Avenue, Miami, FL 33174 — 305-559-6715

HAWAII

1143 Bishop Street, Honolulu, HI 96813 — 808-521-2731

ILLINOIS

172 North Michigan Avenue, Chicago, IL 60601 — 312-346-4228

LOUISIANA

4403 Veterans Memorial Blvd, Metairie, LA 70006 — 504-887-7631

MASSACHUSETTS

885 Providence Hwy, Dedham, MA 02026 — 781-326-5385

MISSOURI

9804 Watson Road, St. Louis, MO 63126 — 314-965-3512

NEW YORK

115 E. 29th Street, New York City, NY 10016 — 212-754-1110

SOUTH CAROLINA

243 King Street, Charleston, SC 29401 — 843-577-0175

TEXAS

No book center; for parish exhibits or outreach evangelization, contact: 210-569-0500, or SanAntonio@paulinemedia.com, or P.O. Box 761416, San Antonio, TX 78245

VIRGINIA

1025 King Street, Alexandria, VA 22314 — 703-549-3806

CANADA

3022 Dufferin Street, Toronto, ON M6B 3T5 — 416-781-9131

¡También somos su fuente para libros, videos y música en español!